CACAO CEREMONIES WITH SOUL

All you need to create sacred and meaningful cacao rituals that open the heart and deepen spiritual connection.

MERCEDES CADARSO SANCHEZ

MARIA SOCASTRO GONZALEZ

The Wing Book

1st edition: November 2024

Revised edition: April 2026

Title: Cacao Ceremonies with soul

I am sending this book out into the world with a big thank you to my friends, who keep me going with their encouragement. To my daughter Lorena, my son Guillermo, and the little sunshine in my life, my granddaughter Kerene, who thinks I am the funniest mom and grandma they could ask for. Thanks to each of you for being such a special part of my life!

Mercedes

I dedicate this book to my daughter Noa, for reminding me that each day is a unique experience, full of wonderful and awe-inspiring moments. Thank you for teaching me to see the world with fresh eyes and to rediscover magic in every step along the way. And to my friend Mercedes, with whom I share this project, for being my unwavering support and encouragement.

Maria

But above all, we thank the spirit of Cacao for allowing us to share its wisdom with such joy and love.

PROLOGUE

Cacao is so much more than just food; it is a sacred vehicle for connecting the body, mind, and spirit, helping us access deeper levels of presence and connection. This manual you hold in your hands offers a doorway into that universe, where the cacao ceremony creates spaces for inner transformation and expansion of the self.

The purpose of this book is to share with you the art of cacao ceremonies—ancestral practices that have been used for centuries to open the heart, heal the soul, and reconnect with our highest essence.

Throughout these pages, we invite you on a journey of mindfulness, where each cacao ceremony becomes a sacred act that raises your vibration and aligns you with the medicine of cacao as a tool for healing and personal growth.

One of the key elements in these ceremonies is medicine music—sounds that accompany and deepen the experience, helping transcend the physical and enter a space of higher connection. You'll also discover the concept of *Tlamanalli,* the sacred offering in the Nahuatl tradition, where cacao becomes a gift to the spirit, a form of gratitude and communion with the elements and life itself.

The benefits of integrating cacao celebrations into your life are profound. This ritual not only opens the heart but also raises your state of consciousness, allowing you to cultivate introspection, mental clarity, and connection with the divine. Through cacao, you can release tensions, heal emotional wounds, and find a space of peace and balance, while celebrating life from a place of openness and gratitude.

As you read this manual, you will learn to:

- Create your own Cacao Ceremonies, tailored to your intention and the energy of the moment, with the power to raise your personal experience.
- Connect with Medicine Music to increase the transformative power of the ritual.
- Incorporate the Tlamanalli as a practice of gratitude and offering, deepening your spiritual connection and aligning with all that is sacred.
- Open your heart to new forms of love, gratitude, and deep connection with yourself and others, celebrating cacao as a life teacher.

This book is more than a practical guide for conducting cacao ceremonies; it is an invitation to a spiritual journey of self-discovery and celebration. It accompanies you on the path of healing and expansion of your being through cacao—that silent teacher that reminds us that love and gratitude are the true paths.

CHAPTER 1

DISCOVERING CACAO

1.1 The cacao tree or cacaotero

The cacao tree thrives in warm, humid climates. It is an evergreen tree that is always in bloom, growing between 6 and 15 meters in height. It needs shade, which is provided by taller trees like coconut palms, banana trees, cedar, and mahogany, among others.

The soil should be rich in nitrogen and potassium, and the climate must be humid, with temperatures ranging between 20°C and 30°C.

Its small pink flowers and fruits grow in an unusual way, directly from the trunk and oldest branches. These flowering plants have a lifespan of 48 hours and are both male and female.

The flowers are pollinated by tiny flies. The fruit is a berry called pod, "maraca" or "vaina", shaped like an elongated zucchini, measuring between 15 to 30cm in length and 7 to 12 cm in width. It can be red, yellow, or purple in color, and weighs about 450 grams when ripe.

In a year, when it matures, it can produce up to 6,000 flowers, but only 20 pods are harvested from them. Despite the fruits ripening year-round, there are typically two harvests: the main one, which begins towards the end of the rainy season and continues into the start of the dry season, and a secondary harvest at the beginning of the next rainy period.

When the pod is opened, it reveals 30 to 40 cacao beans, which undergo several processes before becoming edible.

A cacao tree has an average lifespan of 40 to 45 years.

1.2 Growth areas and varieties of cacao

Mexico was the first country to grow cacao. When the Spanish brought it to Spain, cacao spread throughout Europe. From there, colonizing countries like France, England, and Belgium introduced it to other parts of the world, such as Africa and Asia.

The cultivation of the cacao tree requires specific climatic conditions, which are found in several countries across the Americas, such as Ecuador, Colombia, Brazil, Peru, the Dominican Republic, Venezuela, Bolivia, Guatemala, and Mexico, as well as in African countries like Ghana, Ivory Coast, the Democratic Republic of Congo, Tanzania, and in Bali, Indonesia.

This diversity of regions give origin to the three main varieties used in chocolate production and in ceremonies:

<u>**Criollo Cacao**</u>

Origin and background: Criollo cacao is the oldest and rarest type, originating from Central and South America, especially in countries like Venezuela, Colombia, Ecuador, Nicaragua, and Mexico. It accounts for only a small percentage of global cacao production (around 5%) due to its susceptibility to disease and low productivity.

Characteristics: It is considered the finest and highest quality cacao, with a delicate and complex flavor profile, featuring floral, fruity, and nutty notes. Its low tannin content makes it less bitter and smoother compared to other types of cacao.

Uses: Due to its superior flavor, Criollo cacao is mainly used in the production of gourmet and high-end chocolates. It is highly appreciated in the chocolate industry for its refined taste and distinctive aroma.

Forastero Cacao

Origin and background: Forastero cacao is the most common type, representing the majority of global cacao production (around 80-90%). It is native to the Amazon region but is now widely cultivated in West Africa (Ivory Coast, Ghana, Nigeria, and Cameroon), as well as in Brazil and Ecuador.

Characteristics: This type of cacao is robust, with a stronger and bitter flavor profile, featuring earthy and astringent notes. It is more resistant to disease and has a higher productivity, making it more economical to cultivate.

Uses: It is primarily used in mass chocolate production and sweet products due to its availability and lower cost. It is often blended with Criollo or Trinitario cacao to enhance its flavor profile.

Trinitario Cacao

Origin and background: Trinitario cacao is a hybrid of Criollo and Forastero types, originating in Trinidad in the 18th century. It is cultivated in various regions, including the Caribbean, Central America, Venezuela, and some parts of Asia (Sri Lanka, Papua New Guinea).

Characteristics: It combines the qualities of both Criollo and Forastero, resulting in a balanced flavor profile that can range from floral and fruity to earthy and bitter. It is more disease-resistant than Criollo and has higher productivity.

Uses: Thanks to its balance of flavor and resilience, Trinitario cacao is popular in the production of high-quality chocolates and is appreciated by both chocolatiers and discerning consumers.

The cacaotero tree

National (Arriba)

Origin and background: National cacao, also known as Arriba, is a unique variety from Ecuador. It is cultivated in the regions of Guayas and Manabí.

Characteristics: It has a floral and fruity flavor profile, with notes of jasmine and nuts. It is highly prized for its complexity and distinctive aroma.

Uses: Used in fine and gourmet chocolates, Nacional cacao is the favorite choice for products that stand out for their exceptional flavor and quality.

Madagascar Cacao

Origin and background: Madagascar is famous for its fine cacao, especially the Trinitario variety. It is cultivated in the Sambirano region, in the northwest of the island.

Characteristics: Known for its fruity flavor profile, citrus notes, red berries, and slight acidity. Its unique acidity and brightness stand out from other types of cacao.

Uses: This cacao is used in premium chocolates and is highly valued by artisan chocolatiers for its vibrant and distinctive flavor.

1.3 The influence of Terroir on cacao

Just like wine, the *terroir* (the geographical, climatic, and soil conditions of a region) plays a crucial role in cacao's flavor. The same variety of cacao can have a different flavor profile depending on where it's grown.

Factors like altitude, temperature, humidity, and farming practice affect the chemical compounds in cacao, resulting in a range of unique flavors and aromas.

In summary, the world of cacao is vast and diverse, with each type and variety offering a unique sensory experience. From the delicate and complex Criollo cacao to the robust and common Forastero, and the balanced Trinitario, each has its place in the rich tradition of chocolate-making.

Understanding the different types of cacao and their origins allows us to deeply appreciate the art and science behind every cacao base product we enjoy.

As we explore and taste these different cacaos, we connect with an ancient tradition that celebrates the diversity and richness of this incredible gift from nature.

1.4 Differences in cacao for ceremonies

Any of the three main types of cacao are suitable for cacao ceremonies, as they all contain the same bioactive compounds and provide the same benefits and outcomes.

The choice of one variety over another depends on factors like:

1. The availability of varieties in your area.

2. Your budget, as prices can vary significantly between different varieties and even their origin. The most expensive variety is Trinitario, and within it, the most highly valued comes from the Maracaibo region in Venezuela.

3. Personal taste, as the soil where it is grown gives each variety special characteristics. A Criollo cacao from Ecuador has a different aroma than one from Ivory Coast. Someone might prefer the Ecuadorian variety, while another's palate enjoys the one from Ivory Coast more.

4. The intention of the ceremony you're performing. When choosing a cacao for ceremonies, it is important to consider its geographical origin. Each region brings its own magic to cacao, offering a variety of experiences to meet individual needs and preferences. For example:

Central and south America: These regions, including countries like Ecuador, Peru, and Venezuela, are known for producing high-quality Criollo and Trinitario cacaos. These cacaos often offer complex flavor profiles with fruity, floral, and earthy notes. They are ideal for ceremonies that seek a refined and deep experience of spiritual connection.

West Africa: Countries like Ivory Coast and Ghana: dominate global cacao production, primarily of the Forastero type. This cacao tends to have a stronger, earthier flavor with bitter and roasted notes. It's a popular choice for ceremonies that seek grounded and earthy energy.

Caribbean: In countries like the Dominican Republic and Jamaica, high-quality Criollo cacao is produced, combining the finesse of Criollo with the tropical influence of the Caribbean. These cacaos often offer smooth and fruity flavors, ideal for ceremonies seeking a sensorially rich and exuberant experience.

However, generally speaking, Criollo or Trinitario cacao is often used in ceremonies due to its symbolic value, its association with the sacred, and its more delicate and complex flavor profile.

Furthermore, if it is hard to find these varieties in your area and Forastero cacao is more affordable, you can add infusions, spices, or essential oils that align with the intention of your celebration.

Remember, all cacao contains the same active ingredients, though in different proportions, and this sacred plant offers its fruits for our highest benefit and purposes. Every cacao is magical!

Cacao varieties can be found in different forms: liquid, bites, bars, or powder.

And just like with everything else, there are facilitators who are strong advocates for the bar form, making its preparation a ritual in itself by slicing thin pieces and slowly melting them in a liquid base over a gentle fire.

In the West, this presentation is harder to find and, in our opinion, completely unnecessary. We work with cacao powder because we find it more convenient for weighing and handling.

We mostly use Forastero cacao because it is the easiest to find in Spain, and our palate has grown accustomed to it. But we really love them all, and when we travel and find varieties from other countries, we always bring back a couple of kilos in our suitcase— our whole family loves a good cup of cacao!

1.5 Cacao production process

The cacao production process, from harvesting the pod to obtaining a fine powder, consists of 12 stages. However, it's worth mentioning that cacao can already be used for food and other purposes from stage 8 onward.

These are the phases, though the names may vary depending on the country of origin:

Harvesting the cacao pods

Cacao pods are harvested by hand when they are fully ripe. Harvesting cacao is a difficult task that requires skilled hands.

The cacao production process

Careful selection of the fruit stem is necessary, and it must be removed with a sharp knife without damaging the flowers. This is because cacao pods grow from fertilized flowers, and cacao flowers tend to cluster in what we call a "floral cushion."

The spot where a pod has grown is the same area where new flowers will bloom the following year. If you cut or damage that area, you create a wound, and the tree will avoid blooming there, which would reduce productivity.

Manual harvesting ensures that only ripe pods are picked, improving the quality of the cacao.

Extracting the beans

The harvester places the pods in a basket and brings them to a central area within the Cacao Farm.

Once there, two workers sit facing each other with a wooden board between them and use a dull machete to break open the pod.

The pods are opened to extract the cacao beans and the white pulp surrounding them. This "de-podding" is done by hand and requires a large workforce.

Proper extraction of the beans allows the fermentation process to begin, which is crucial for developing the flavor.

Fermentation

The purpose of fermentation is to remove the sticky pulp surrounding the bean and to kill the embryo, preventing it from swelling and spoiling the fruit.

Fermentation reduces the astringency and bitterness of the bean, as it breaks down sugars and starches into acids and alcohol.

The beans are fermented in wooden boxes the same day they are harvested. Farmers ensure that no infected beans, such as those with "witches' broom" disease, are found during the process, and any affected beans are discarded.

"The beans are fermented in wooden boxes the same day they are harvested. When filling the boxes, producers check that the beans do not have a fungus called 'Witches Broom'. If diseased beans are found during the process, the affected grains are removed."

It is extremely important for the boxes to be fully filled. Fermentation begins when the sugars start to concentrate, and the temperature rises, reaching 58C.

The next morning, the cacao is transferred from one box to another, a process known as 'rotation.' Using wooden paddles, the beans are stirred and moved between boxes.

Once rotated, the top of the box is covered with banana leaves, ensuring there are no gaps where air can enter, preventing the beans from oxidizing. The beans remain covered for 48 hours. After this period, they are rotated again, covered once more, and rotated every 24 hours for at least six days.

During fermentation, the pulp drips off the cacao beans, which is why the fermentation boxes have holes for the pulp to drain out. About 33% of the wet weight of the cacao is lost after fermentation, which is quite significant.

At the end of the process, the pulp is removed, and what the cacao farmers refer to as the "precursors" of aroma is developed which enhances the flavor of the cacao.

At the end of this process, the pulp is removed, and as the cacao farmers say, the "precursors" of aroma arise which enhances the flavor of the cacao.

Drying

Finally, after the long fermentation process, the beans are ready to be dried. This is another crucial step in improving the flavor of cacao.

Cacao is dried in wooden boxes, beds, platforms, or patios for about a week. During this drying stage, the moisture content is reduced from 60% to 7%, preventing mold and stopping the fermentation process, thus preserving the flavors. As with coffee, it is important to turn the beans periodically to ensure equal drying.

At this point, the cacao can already be used for various food products, but it is usually taken to the next phase.

Roasting

Just like coffee, cacao does not fully release its flavors or develop its rich brown color until it's roasted. This process is very sensitive.

In the past, this was done with large rotating spheres, during a specific time and temperature. Depending on the variety of cacao, the roasting process, time, and temperature vary.

The beans are roasted slowly, between 25 and 50 minutes at around 110°C to 150°C. Once the temperature and time are reached, a specialist's nose determines the optimal moment to stop the process, ensuring the beans do not over-carbonize. If necessary, forced ventilation is used to cool the beans and prevent spoilage.

This process brings out the characteristic chocolate flavor, with notes of nuts and fruit, depending on the variety. These flavors and aromas are what chocolate experts love.

It also facilitates the separation of the shell and removes some of the volatile acids present in cacao (like acetic acid), giving the beans a less acidic taste.

Peeling

The roasted beans are broken, and the shells are removed to obtain cacao nibs, which are the base for producing cacao powder.

Grinding

The roasted beans are circulated through a series of mills. During this grinding process, the cellular structure of the beans, which contains 50% to 60% cacao butter, is broken down, releasing much of the butter.

This liquefied butter forms a fluid paste known as cacao liquor.

Pressing

The cacao liquor is subjected to intense pressure to separate the cacao butter. What remains is known as cacao paste.

Cacao butter is used in fine pastries, giving chocolate its special shine. It is also used to make white chocolate and cosmetics, as it nourishes and protects the skin from dehydration.

Crushing

The cacao paste is broken into small pieces to make it easier to handle in the next step, which is grinding.

Crushing ensures smooth processing and helps turn cacao into a uniform powder.

Fine grinding

The crushed cacao pieces are ground to obtain cacao powder.

Sifting

The cacao powder is sifted to remove lumps and achieve a homogeneous texture, producing fine, smooth, high-quality cacao, suitable for various culinary applications and beverages.

Packaging

The cacao powder, or any of its other forms, is packaged in airtight containers for storage and distribution. This preserves its freshness and quality, protecting it from moisture and contaminants.

Each of these phases is essential to ensure that cacao reaches our tables in the highest possible quality. This is how cacao becomes the delicious powder we use in our cacao ceremonies!

1.6 Cacao presentations

Cacao comes in various forms, each offering different applications in cooking and baking, allowing for the creation of a wide variety of products and dishes, as shown in the following table:

PRESENTATION	DESCRIPTION	USES
Cacao Paste	It is the edible part of the cacao bean, and is the result of grinding roasted cacao beans at high temperatures to be liquid, pouring it into molds where it solidifies. It has a strong bitter taste and is difficult to digest.	**Pastry:** Base for maker choc:late bonbons and other chocolate confections. **Cooking:** Ingredient in sauces and marinades. Ideal to balance recipes with an excessive amount of sugar.
Cacao Powder	Obtained by pressing cacao paste to extract cacao butter. The solid residue is good to form a fine powder.	**Drinks:** Hot chocolate, milk shakes. **Pastry:** Cakes, cookies, brownies, etc. **Cooking:** Salty dishes like mole sauce, highly apprecíited in Mexio for meats and fish, gourmet.
Cacao Liquor	Also known as cacao liquor, it is the result of grinding roasted cacao beans. It has a liquid texture when hot and solidifies when cooled.	**Pastry:** Base for making dark chocolate, milk chocolate, white chocolate, and truffles. **Cooking:** Sauces and gourmet preparations.
Cacao Butter	Natural fat extracted from roasted cacao beans. It is yellowish in color and makes up 55% of the bean mass.	**Pastry:** Base for making white chocolate, milk chocolate, white chocolate, and truffles. **Cooking:** Sauces and gourmet preparations.
Cacao Nibs	Fragments of roasted cacao beans, peeled and broken into small pieces, with a rough texture and an intense bitter taste.	**Snacks:** Add to cereals, yogurt, smoothies. **Cooking:** Salads, granola, to garnish a gourmet dish.

1.7 Cacao name

"Theobroma Cacao" is the scientific name of the cacao tree, an evergreen plant from the Malvaceae family.

The name *Theobroma Cacao* was coined by the Swedish naturalist Carl Linnaeus in the 18th century.

Theobroma comes from Greek and means "food of the gods," while "cacao" has its roots in the languages of Mesoamerican civilizations, particularly in Nahuatl, where it was called "cacahuatl." This word was adapted by the Spanish during the conquest of the Americas, becoming "cacao."

1.8 The legend of cacao

The most widespread legend about how cacao reached humans involves the god Quetzalcóatl, known as the "Feathered Serpent," one of the most important deities in Mesoamerican mythology, especially among the Aztecs and Toltecs. Quetzalcóatl was revered as the god of wisdom, wind, fertility, creation, and a symbol of life.

According to the legend, Quetzalcóatl decided to gift cacao to humans, a sacred plant that only the gods could enjoy because he was moved by the devotion and hard work of humans.

Quetzalcóatl stole the plant from the garden of the gods and planted it in the human world, teaching them how to harvest cacao and prepare a sacred drink that was bitter and mixed with spices.

This legend highlights the importance of cacao in Mesoamerican cosmology, known as "the drink of the gods," and was reserved for the elite, for special occasions, and was even used as currency.

This divine offering granted humans wisdom and strength, becoming a symbol of gratitude and respect toward Quetzalcóatl.

The feather serpent of Quetzalcóatl

However, the other gods were enraged when they discovered that Quetzalcóatl had shared this divine gift with humans. Despite their anger, Quetzalcóatl's action ensured that cacao became an integral part of Mesoamerican culture and life.

They prepared it with water and spices, sweetened with honey, and it wasn't until the Spaniards brought it to Spain that it started being prepared with cow's milk.

Over time, cacao spread around the world, becoming one of the most popular and cherished products worldwide, with many uses from beverages to chocolates and beauty products.

Even today, cacao remains a powerful symbol of the rich history and roots of Mesoamerican culture. Every time a cup of cacao is prepared or enjoyed, its identity and legacy as "the drink of the gods" are honored, along with its many beneficial attributes.

Most people in Mesoamerica continue the tradition of drinking it with water rather than milk, staying true to its ancestral origins.

1.9 Key characteristics of Cacao

Cacao is much more than a delicious food; it is a sacred plant with an ancient of comprehensive benefits that encompass physical, emotional, mental, and spiritual well-being.

Let us dive into the multiple benefits of cacao and discover how it can enrich all aspects of your life.

Physiological benefits of cacao

Cacao also has a long history as a medicinal plant, used to treat various ailments and improve overall health.

Pre-Hispanic cultures believed it had nourishing, strengthening properties, and even served as a potent aphrodisiac.

In traditional medicine, it was used to aid digestion, boost energy, reduce fatigue, and as a treatment for abdominal pain, fever, and other conditions.

Today, scientific studies have identified cacao as being rich in antioxidants and other bioactive compounds that can benefit heart health, improve blood circulation, and have anti-inflammatory and neuroprotective effects.

Cacao is a true nutritional treasure, rich in various beneficial compounds. Here is a detailed breakdown of its average composition per one hundred grams of cacao powder:

The content of phenylethylamine and anandamide in cacoa is relatively low compared to other compounds, but their presence is significant due to their effects on mood and the sense of well-being.

Here approximates their concentrations and effects:"

Cacao – Nutritional Composition & Key Components	
Calories:	228 kcal
Water:	5 mg
Proteins:	19.6 g
Fats:	13.7 g
Saturated:	8.1 g
Monounsaturrated:	4.6 g
Polyunsaturated:	0.4 g
Carbohydrates:	57.9 g
Sugars:	1.8 g
Dietary Fiber:	37.0 g
Minerals:	3.5 mg
Iron:	13.9 mg (77% of the Recommended Daily Value – DV)
Magnesium:	499 mg (125% of the DV)
Phosphorus:	734 mg (105% of the DV)
Potassium:	1,524 mg (32% of the DV)
Zinc:	6.8 mg (62% of the DV)
Vitamins:	
Vitamin E:	0.1 mg (1% of the DV)
Vitamin B1 (Thiamine):	0.1 mg (6% of the DV)
Vitamin B2 (Riboflavin):	0.2 mg (12% of the DV)
Vitamin B3 (Niacin):	2.2 mg (11% of the DV)
Vitamin B6:	0.1 mg (6% of the DV)
Other Important Components:	<ul><li>**Phenylethylamine:** 0.4 – 6.6 mg/g</li><li>**Anandamide:** nanograms/g</li><li>**Theobromine**</li><li>**Flavonoids**</li></ul>

Phenylethylamine

Phenylethylamine is an organic compound that acts as a neurotransmitter and is known for its mood-enhancing effects. The concentration of phenylethylamine in cacao is approximately 0.4-6.6 mg per gram of cacao powder.

Although the amount is small, phenylethylamine, also known as the "love molecule," can influence the release of dopamine and endorphins, improve mood and promote a sense of happiness.

Anandamide

Anandamide is an endocannabinoid naturally produced by the body and found in small amounts in cacao. The concentration of anandamide in cacao is much lower, typically in the range of nanograms per gram of cacao.

Despite its low concentration, anandamide can interact with cannabinoid receptors in the brain, promoting a sense of well-being and happiness like the effects produced by cannabinoids in cannabis, though in a much milder way.

It acts as a key regulator of brain functions such as mood, promoting contained euphoria, ecstasy and enhancing memory. Additionally, it helps regulate hunger, sleep patterns and pain relief.

Theobromine

Known for its mild stimulating effect, theobromine promotes alertness and mental clarity without the adverse side effects associated with caffeine.

Combined Effects

Although the concentrations of phenylethylamine and anandamide in cacao are small, their effects are amplified by other compounds found in cacao, such as theobromine and flavonoids.

These compounds work together to boost mood, reduce stress, and promote an overall sense of well-being. Incorporating cacao consciously and in balance into your diet can offer a variety of positive effects for both body and mind.

However, it is important not to confuse cacao with chocolate, as they are not the same product. Cacao becomes chocolate after a process in which a lot of sugar, and in most cases, milk, is added, reducing the percentage of cacao and introducing ingredients that are not particularly healthy.

Always look for products that contain at least 75% cacao, whether in chocolate bars, powdered drinks, or baking bars, and add healthier sweeteners like honey, agave, stevia, or even xylitol (birch sugar).

CHAPTER 2

THE BENEFITS OF CACAO

2.1 The impact of ceremonies

In a world that is increasingly fast-paced and technological, many people are rediscovering the magic of ancestral practices and traditional ceremonies to find balance and well-being. But how effective are these ceremonies for our mind and heart?

Recent research has shown that rituals and ceremonies have wonderful effects on our mental and emotional health. These effects are not just anecdotal; there is a scientific base supporting their benefits.

It has been proven that when you induce the brain to vibrate at the frequency of delta waves, which are slow, powerful waves (between 0.5 Hz and 4 Hz), numerous benefits are generated, not only physically but also spiritually.

Delta waves are predominant during deep, restorative sleep, specifically in stage 3 of non-REM sleep, also known as slow-wave sleep. During this stage, the body carries out vital processes of regeneration and recovery, while also opening the door to spiritual experiences and altered states of consciousness.

The presence of delta waves is associated with the release of important hormones like growth hormones, which plays a crucial role in tissue repair and muscle growth. However, from a spiritual perspective, these waves allow for a deeper connection with the inner self and higher planes of existence.

In deep sleep, meditation, and in these types of rituals, delta wave activity is stimulated, which not only fosters a state of calm and reduces stress but also facilitates access to higher levels of consciousness. These altered states of consciousness enable greater perception and understanding of spiritual reality, providing a more intimate connection with the divine, deep insights, and energetic healing.

Furthermore, delta waves have been shown to strengthen the immune system, and from a holistic perspective, they help balance and harmonize the body's energy fields.

During the ritual, the increase in cytokine production not only aids in fighting infections but is also perceived as energetic cleansing and a rebalancing of chakras and the body's energy fields.

There is also research indicating that the gut contains a mass of nerves that function like a second brain. This means our intestine is a reliable source of intuition when making decisions.

During a cacao ceremony, the ingestion of cacao directly activates the release of neurotransmitters and endorphins through the gut which not only improves mood but also promotes a state of deep meditation and spiritual connection.

This state facilitates access to the subconscious mind, where a vast amount of information and wisdom resides. Participating in a cacao ceremony allows for a deep intuitive connection, enabling decisions to be made not just from logic and conscious thought but also from intuition and inner wisdom.

Your unconscious mind holds much more information than your conscious mind. When you make decisions based solely on logic and consciousness, you miss the vast capacity of the subconscious brain. The cacao ceremony is a powerful way to integrate this internal wisdom, connecting body, mind, and spirit.

This ancestral practice not only honors the tradition and benefits of cacao but also provides a sacred space to listen to and trust the signals that our body sends us, allowing for more holistic and aligned decision-making with our true self.

Interior Cacao Ceremony

2.2 Well-being and social connection

Cacao not only offers spiritual benefits but also provides a wide range of physical, emotional, and social advantages, some of which are detailed below:

Physical well-being: Cacao ceremonies reduce stress and improve mood by strengthening the immune system and lowering blood pressure. This is achieved by decreasing cortisol levels, the hormone linked to stress.

Social connection: Ceremonies and rituals are typically performed in groups, fostering a deep sense of belonging and community. This feeling of social connection is crucial for maintaining mental and emotional health, as isolation is associated with higher rates of depression, anxiety, and other physical, emotional, and mental ailments.

Mood improvement: Participating in celebrations can release endorphins, the happiness hormone. These events can be especially helpful during times of grief or loss, providing a space to process emotions and find comfort.

Increased resilience: Rituals help us face challenges and difficult transitions. By providing structure and a symbolic framework, ceremonies can bring meaning to experiences that might otherwise feel chaotic or traumatic.

Mindfulness practice: Many rituals require full focus and presence in the moment, making them an effective way to practice mindfulness.

Mental clarity and creativity: The repetition and structure of rituals can create a mental state where ideas flow more freely, promoting creativity and problem-solving.

Personal fulfillment: Celebrations offer a sense of achievement and fulfillment, especially those that mark important life milestones.

Emotional balance: Rituals help regulate emotions by providing a safe space to express and process them.

2.3 Origin of the cacao ceremony

The history of cacao as a ceremonial elixir began over 3,000 years ago in the heart of Mesoamerica. The Mayans cultivated cacao trees with meticulous care, aware of their healing properties on a physical, emotional, and spiritual level.

Cacao was reserved for special celebrations, as it was believed that it allowed communication with higher planes, a greater state of consciousness and guidance from the spiritual world.

Thus, cacao was passed down from generation to generation, from culture to culture, until the Spanish colonization. The Spaniards, attracted to its flavor, brought it to Europe, and from there, it spread worldwide.

While Europeans appreciated the taste of cacao, they paid little attention to its ceremonial and spiritual roots. The sacred nature of cacao, as understood by Indigenous cultures, was overshadowed by its commercial value and its appeal as a luxury drink.

The rebirth of cacao

It was not until the mid-20th century that cacao ceremonies experienced a revival. This resurgence was driven by renewed interest in Indigenous traditions and the use of spiritual plants.

Today, many practitioners around the world are rediscovering the ancient wisdom of cacao, embracing it as a powerful tool for personal and collective transformation.

Cacao ceremony today

Modern cacao ceremonies are inspired by traditional practices while incorporating contemporary elements and influences from other cultures that preserve ancestral traditions, such as the Hindu tradition.

Facilitators guide participants through various rituals that combine cacao consumption with meditation, breathwork, mindfulness exercises, and group sharing.

These ceremonies are designed to open the heart, explore the inner self, and promote a sense of unity and interconnectedness. We are not alone; we are a community of humans supporting each other on our evolutionary path.

The spirit of cacao continues to inspire a growing community of individuals seeking connection with themselves and the world around them. These ceremonies offer a unique experience that can transform both body and spirit.

By immersing yourself in this celebration, you can appreciate the diverse benefits resulting from the active ingredients present in cacao. In these pages, we show you how these ingredients work and why attending a cacao ceremony can be a deeply enriching experience.

Living tradition testimonials

Recently, I had the chance to speak with one of the few women dedicated to making mezcal in Oaxaca, Mexico. Mezcal is an ancient and exclusive alcoholic drink with a complex production process, as part of the agave or maguey plant must be cooked, fermented, and distilled by hand.

This variety of agave grows wild between rocks, and its mystical and physical properties are unmatched for the spirit and body.

This precious 38-year-old woman told me she was going through a painful grieving process because her father had died, and she had taken over the mezcal factory, feeling disoriented and unsure of how to proceed, which made her feel insecure.

I suggested she attend therapy, and she said she already did. Every Sunday, the women in her family—her grandmother, mother, aunts, sisters, and cousins—gathered at home to prepare food while drinking a cup of cacao and venting their problems, receiving advice from the older women. What better therapy than that!

Honoring ancestors through cacao

Cacao is like an ointment that helps us heal and regain our well-being. Its properties make us feel safe to open our hearts and receive help. The idea of "giving and receiving" is essential: what you give comes back. If you want a life full of abundance and prosperity, start by being generous.

The history of cacao ceremonies is fascinating, a tapestry woven with ancestral respect, colonial influences, and modern rediscovery. Participating in a cacao ceremony today is a way of honoring the legacy of our ancestors. Cacao is more than a delicacy; it is a sacred companion on our journey toward higher consciousness, spiritual awakening, and holistic well-being.

When we immerse ourselves in the experience of cacao, we remember the importance of honoring our roots and traditions. It helps keep the spirit of our ancestral cultures alive and opens us to love and connection with everything around us. May each sip of cacao be an offering of gratitude and a step toward a more conscious and united world.

2.4 Fusion of ancestral and modern practices

The saying "past is always better" does not reflect our beliefs. We believe in the richness of the past but also in the innovation of the present. We rescue the best of ancestral traditions and blend them with contemporary research and techniques, creating a cacao celebration that is both complete and modern.

Our ceremony honors the wisdom of ancient cultures while benefiting from modern advancements, offering an enriching and transformative experience that resonates with the spirit and needs of today.

Guiding each personality toward wholeness

According to the Enneagram, people tend to function from three different centers or approaches, which influences their perception of life and how they focus their attention to meet certain needs.

Recognizing this diversity, we explain all the necessary steps to conduct an excellent cacao ceremony, ensuring that each participant, regardless of their personality type, experiences a sense of satisfaction, wholeness, and happiness.

2.5 The 3 centers according to the enneagram

The three types of centers and their characteristics are as follows:

Instinctive center

These individuals need to control their comfort and manage their internal and external sensations to feel safe. We offer activities that reinforce their sense of protection of their sensations, such as providing detailed information about what their body might experience during the celebration.

It is crucial to respect their timing and privacy without forcing them to participate in the sharing moments.

They experience the ceremony from the present, enjoying the here and now.

Emotional center

These individuals need to be moved by what they do. We offer practices that connect with their emotions, such as guided meditation that allows them to experience the emotions that arise in the moment.

It is important to allow them to express their emotions and to value the sharing of their feelings without judgment or commenting on their experience.

They experience the ceremony from the past and need to share their emotions from the ceremony to feel understood and valued.

Mental center

These individuals need answers to their questions and to understand the process being carried out. We explain the various steps of the ceremony clearly and concisely.

It is essential to allow them to express their doubts and offer precise and specific answers.

They experience the ceremony anticipating the future impact and need to find practical meaning in the cacao celebration.

2.6 Combining Other Techniques

The integration of holistic therapies such as chromotherapy, aromatherapy, and the use of crystals can amplify the benefits of cacao.

These complementary therapies not only enrich the experience but also address the various emotional, physical, and spiritual needs of the participants.

> **Chromotherapy:** The use of color in the altar or ceremonial space helps energize our chakras, which are the energy centers or "batteries of our body."

> **Aromatherapy:** The use of specific essential oils creates a unique personal and environmental atmosphere for the ceremony.

> **Crystals:** Placing crystals around the ceremonial space can amplify the energy and provide additional energetic balance.

> **Sound therapy:** Using instruments like Tibetan or crystal bowls, tuning forks, or other sound instruments facilitates deep relaxation and spiritual connection.

> **Body exercises:** Incorporating postures to stretch the body and breathing exercises help release tension and promote a deeper connection with oneself.

> **Guided meditation:** Leading participants through visualizations and guided meditation deepens the spiritual and emotional experience.

> **Herbal medicine:** Applying principles from this ancient science, such as adding herbs and spices to the cacao, enhances the healing aspect of the cacao.

Each of these therapies and many others bring their own unique benefits, and when combined with the cacao ceremony, they create a holistic experience that addresses multiple dimensions of being.

This integration allows participants not only to enjoy the present moment but also to explore and heal different aspects of their emotional, physical, and spiritual lives.

2.7 From ancestral to modern

While we have modernized certain aspects of the ceremony, it is also crucial to preserve the ancestral practices that honor the tradition of cacao. These practices not only preserve the cultural and spiritual richness of the ritual but also deepen participants' connection to the sacred essence of cacao.

Below are some of the ancestral practices that can be incorporated into cacao ceremonies:

Storytelling about Cacao

Telling the story of Cacao's origins is a fundamental part of the ceremony. Sharing the history and spirituality behind Cacao not only educates participants but also helps them understand and respect the importance of the ritual.

These stories may include tales of how cacao was discovered and used by ancient Mesoamerican civilizations, the myths and legends associated with its spiritual power, and the traditions of Indigenous peoples who have revered cacao as a sacred plant for centuries.

Altar/Tlamanalli

Creating an altar, known in some traditions as "Tlamanalli", is a practice that strengthens the spiritual connection during the ceremony. An altar may include elements such as flowers, seeds, feathers, minerals, candles, and figures of deities or spiritual symbols.

Each element in the altar has meaning and purpose, helping to channel the energy and intentions of the ceremony. The creation of the altar is an act of reverence and gratitude toward the earth and establishes a sacred space where participants can focus their attention and devotion.

A crystal quartz as the center of the Tlamanalli

Connection with nature

Whenever possible, holding the ceremony in a natural environment can intensify the experience and connect participants with the energy of the earth. Nature acts as a catalyst that amplifies the energies of the ceremony, providing an atmosphere that is both calming and revitalizing.

Participants may feel a deeper connection with natural elements such as air, water, earth, and fire, allowing them to immerse themselves more fully in the ritual. The presence of trees, rivers, and other natural elements can create a sense of harmony and balance, enhancing the healing effects of cacao.

2.8 Other ancestral practices

Chants and mantras: Incorporating traditional chants and mantras during the ceremony can help elevate the vibration of the space and unite participants in a common frequency of intention and spirituality.

Ritual dance: Dance is a powerful way to express and release energy. Including ritual dances can help participants connect with their bodies and the earth's energy, facilitating a deeper and more transformative experience.

Guided meditation: Leading participants through guided meditations that focus on connecting with cacao and nature, allowing them to explore their inner world and release emotional blockages.

Offerings: Making offerings to the earth and spirits is a practice of gratitude and reciprocity. These offerings can include food, flowers, and other symbolic items representing gratitude and respect toward the earth and spiritual forces.

Integrating these ancestral practices into the cacao ceremony not only enriches participants' experiences but also preserves and honors the spiritual traditions passed down through generations.

By keeping this connection to the past alive while incorporating modern elements, we create a ritual that is both respectful of its roots and relevant to our time. In doing so, we cultivate a deep reverence for nature and the sacred practices that nourish our soul and spirit.

CHAPTER 3
PRE-CEREMONY STEPS

3.1 Ideal dates for ceremonies

Cacao's energy is feminine and harmonizes with the lunar cycle. You do not need to be an expert in astrology to benefit from the moon's energy; a simple almanac indicating lunar phases and zodiac signs is enough to plan your ceremonies.

As a facilitator, choose dates of growth and expansion, as each celebration is a seed you plant for the participants' dreams to blossom.

New moons, waxing moons, and full moons are ideal for these celebrations because the energy is at its peak for manifesting desires. Avoid waning moons, as their energy is more introspective and less conducive to expansion.

The lunar influence lasts from three days before to three days after its phase, giving you a seven-day window to hold your celebration, ideally over the weekend when it's easier for people to attend.

The cacao ceremony is convened with a specific goal, theme, or intention, and at this point, it is essential to inform the attendees about the significance of what will be addressed in this ceremony. This is the reason these people have gathered today.

If you have convened the ceremony, it is because you believe the topic is of interest, and you've prepared the theme. There are as many topics as there are ideas, so be creative and prepare a beautiful ceremony that helps raise consciousness, which is what this planet needs.

It is very likely that you are a therapist, instructor, or facilitator in other disciplines and want to incorporate activities or exercises that you usually use because you know the environment they create and their benefits.

This is a great idea. As a professional in your field, you already know the positive impact these practices can have on the physical, mental, and emotional health of your participants. Integrating the cacao ceremony can further enrich these experiences, providing an additional dimension of spiritual connection and well-being.

3.2 Occasions for holding a ceremony

Cacao is a sacred plant known for its spiritual benefits, as it "opens the heart."

By consuming it, we feel more connected to ourselves and others, experiencing feelings of hope, joy, and companionship, reflecting the qualities of the heart.

Cacao ceremonies allow us to deepen this connection, serving as an ideal space to celebrate, reflect, or share a meaningful experience with others.

We offer a basic structure as a guide to help you feel confident in beginning to lead your own cacao ceremonies. However, the most important thing is to apply your own knowledge, creativity, and intuition.

Adapting these suggestions to your personal style and the needs of the participants will make each ceremony unique and reflect your energy and dedication. Make this precious event your own and let the magic of cacao guide you!

The duration of the ceremony should be adjusted to the occasion and the needs of the group, ensuring the experience is fulfilling and meaningful.

There are many ideal occasions for celebrating with cacao, and below we list some of the most common and significant ones, each with a unique spiritual and emotional purpose.

Birth: Celebrate the arrival of a new being into the world by welcoming them with love and good wishes.

Engagement: Bless the union of a couple, wishing them a path filled with happiness and harmony.

Birthdays: Mark the start of a new year of life with the intention of attracting enriching experiences and spiritual growth.

Personal growth: Elevate your personal frequency by facilitating more conscious and aligned decisions.

Ancestral healing: Release inherited burdens by promoting healing and well-being through your lineage.

New moon connection: Tune into the energy of new beginnings and opportunities.

Full moon celebration: Enjoy the fruits and culmination of your efforts.

Seasonal changes: Align your energies with the solstices and equinoxes, flowing with nature's transformations.

Love and connection: Fill yourself with love and share this positive energy with those around you.

At the end of a workshop: If you've planned a multi-hour training workshop, such as yoga, chi-kung, TRE (Tension & Trauma Releasing Exercises), Pilates, or any other physical practice, ending with a cacao ceremony will be enriching.

This will not only help integrate the physical benefits of the workshop but also provide emotional and spiritual closure, allowing participants to leave with a complete and transformative experience.

Spiritual retreat: During a multi-day retreat, a cacao ceremony can be the highlight that unites participants in a moment of deep reflection and connection. It can serve as an opening for the retreat or as a closing that consolidates the experiences obtained.

Group therapy: If you work with groups in therapy sessions, cacao can facilitate emotional openness and communication among group members, creating an environment of trust and mutual support.

Personal celebrations: Anniversaries, birthdays, and engagements are perfect occasions to incorporate a cacao ceremony. This ritual can add a special and meaningful touch to these celebrations, making participants feel honored and connected.

Individual healing sessions: Even in one-on-one sessions, a cacao ceremony can be a powerful tool to help your clients open their hearts and deepen their personal healing process.

3.3 Duration of the ceremony

The length of a cacao ceremony is completely flexible and is in the hands of the facilitator. You decide the length depending on the purpose and the group's energy.

If cacao is the heart of the gathering, the ceremony can be longer; however, if it complements another event, it will be shorter. The key is to adapt to the purpose of the celebration and the participants' needs to create a meaningful experience.

Below, we provide some examples to help you decide the appropriate length based on the occasion.

3.4 The ceremony as a complement

It's likely that you're an instructor of yoga, tai chi, or any other discipline, and at the end of several hours of a workshop, you might want to close the day with a cacao ceremony. In this case, since participants are already tired from all the work done, our suggestion is to keep the ceremony under 40 minutes.

Intention: Provide a calming and comforting way to end the day

Duration: Approximately 40 minutes.

Benefit: Allows participants to relax and absorb the benefits of the workshop without feeling overwhelmed by a long activity.

3.5 Opening or closing ceremony

In emotional therapeutic work with a group, the cacao ceremony can be done either at the beginning or the end of the workshop.

Before the workshop

At the start, you ensure a shift in the participants' energy, making them more open and ready to work more fluidly on the issue of the workshop's theme.

Intention: Prepare participants emotionally and energetically for the therapeutic work.

Duration: Approximately 50 minutes.

Benefit: Facilitates an atmosphere of openness and readiness for emotional work.

After the workshop

To close the workshop, you could offer a cup of cacao while participants share their experiences and expressions of gratitude. This helps to conclude the session harmoniously and reinforces the bonds created during the therapeutic process.

Intention: Close the therapeutic work with group reflection and sharing.

Duration: Approximately 20 minutes.

Benefit: Promotes the integration of the experience and mutual acknowledgment.

3.6 Independent cacao ceremony

If the cacao ceremony is not incorporated into another event, the duration can vary between two and three hours, depending on the theme and intention of the celebration.

This structure allows for a deeper exploration of the practices and rituals associated with cacao, offering a more complete and profound experience.

Intention: Provide a deep and comprehensive experience with cacao.

Duration: 2-3 hours.

Benefit: Allows full immersion in the cacao ritual, including meditations, songs, and reflections.

Remember that cacao ceremony is not just a practice, but an experience that can profoundly transform those who participate.

Your role as a facilitator is essential in guiding and holding this sacred space, ensuring that each person feels supported and connected throughout the process. Trust your intuition and let cacao work its magic!

I hope these ideas inspire you and help you integrate cacao into your professional practices in a meaningful and elevating way. Enjoy creating and facilitating these beautiful ceremonies!

3.7 Activation of the senses in rituals

In any ritual or celebration, the five senses become the protagonists of an experience that goes beyond the physical, transporting us to a deep state of connection and presence.

Through each sense, we can begin an inner journey. This sensory and spiritual experience is enhanced when the ceremonial area is carefully prepared, aligning all elements with the purpose of the ceremony.

Sight: The ceremony begins with the decoration of the ceremonial place, which should be in harmony with the theme and intention of the ceremony. Symbolic objects, soft colors, and natural elements transform the environment, creating a space that invites introspection and spiritual connection.

Additionally, the lighting of the space plays a crucial role: taking advantage of natural light during the day or using dim lights and candles at night can intensify the atmosphere of calm and reverence, preparing the spirit for the experience.

In cacao ceremonies, we are also invited to observe the cacao, the thick brown liquid resting in the cup. Its deep, earthy color immediately connects us to the earth, reminding us of nature's richness.

The ceremony engages all five senses.

Hearing: Sound is a powerful tool in rituals and ceremonies. As we drink, we can listen to the silence around us, broken only by the soft murmur of collective breathing or the ceremonial words of the guide.

The sound of instruments like Tibetan bowls or drums can resonate with the natural rhythm of the cacao, harmonizing the environment and helping participants relax and tune in to the present moment.

Every sound, every whisper, resonates within us, amplifying the connection with the universe.

Smell: Preparing the space with the soft aroma of incense, essential oils, or aromatic herbs also plays a crucial role in this experience. These scents not only prepare the body and mind for the ceremony but also act as a bridge to the sacred space we are creating.

In cacao ceremonies, before drinking, we bring the cup to our nose, allowing the warm, enveloping aroma of the cacao to fill our nostrils.

Its fragrance transports us to the jungles where cacao trees grow, evoking feelings of well-being and connection with the history and spirit of this sacred plant.

Touch: Touch is the physical connection to cacao. Feeling the warmth of the cup in our hands grounds us in the present and makes us aware of our active participation in the ceremony.

Every texture and temperature in our hands reminds us of the energy and effort invested in preparing for this moment. This tactile connection to the sacred drink grounds us in the present, reminding us that we are part of this moment, the circle, and nature itself.

Taste: Taste is the culminating sense in the cacao ceremony. As we bring the cup to our lips, the flavor of the cacao fills our mouth, inviting us to savor each note and nuance with full attention.

This moment is not only for physical enjoyment but also for deep spiritual connection. When consumed mindfully, cacao nourishes not only the body but also the soul, opening our hearts and elevating our energy. Savoring the cacao is an act of communion, an experience that deeply connects us with ourselves and the spirit of this sacred plant.

By integrating all the senses into the cacao ceremony and preparing the space with care and attention, we create a multisensory experience that allows us to connect deeply with ourselves, others, and the sacred essence of cacao.

Each sense is a gateway that takes us beyond the physical, inviting us into a state of full and loving presence, where cacao becomes a vehicle for deep connection and spiritual transformation.

CHAPTER 4

REHEARSAL AND PREPARATION

Before hosting your first official celebration, we highly recommend inviting a couple of trusted people, such as friends and family, to "rehearse" the entire process.

This rehearsal will allow you to better calibrate timing, anticipate possible problem issues, answer potential questions, and make necessary adjustments to your program.

Intention: Ensure the ceremony runs smoothly and that all aspects are well-coordinated.

Benefit: Provides you with the confidence and experience needed to conduct successful ceremonies in the future.

4.1 Benefits of rehearsing the ceremony

1. **Calibrate timing:** Adjust the duration of each segment of the ceremony to ensure it flows naturally and without haste.

2. **Identify potential issues:** Detect and solve potential problems before the official ceremony.
3. **Practice facilitation:** Develop your ability to guide participants through the ceremony with confidence and empathy.
4. **Receive feedback:** Gain valuable insights from friends and family on what worked well and what could be improved.

The duration of a cacao ceremony should be adjusted to the intention and context of the event to ensure an enriching and balanced experience.

Whether as the closure of a workshop, the opening of a therapeutic session, or as an independent event, adapting the time and rehearsing in advance is essential for a successful ceremony and transformative experience.

By paying attention to these details, facilitators can create a space where participants feel safe, supported, and deeply connected.

4.2 Indoor or outdoor ceremonies

There is a difference between being in an outdoor or indoor location or the living room of a home.

Sometimes you can choose where to hold the ceremony, and other times you'll need to adapt to the circumstances, but the essential thing is the intention, dedication, and generosity with which you conduct the cacao ceremony.

Outdoor ceremonies generate a higher energy of joy and happiness than indoor ones but require more planning as the weather is a major factor.

You must be prepared for hot or cold weather or the possibility of unexpected rain. Additionally, insects may be attracted to the flowers of the "Tlamanalli" and the smell of cacao. Everything has its pros and cons—keep this in mind when planning!

4.3 Size of the ceremony space

The amount of space you need is determined by the number of participants and the type of exercises or movements you plan to include.

If you plan a ceremony without movement exercises, then the space required will be smaller. And if it is a small group that will not be lying down, clearly, you'll need even less space. Adapt to what you have and be grateful and enjoy!

4.4 Temperature

Extreme cold or heat can make participants uncomfortable and hinder the smooth flow of the ceremony. Make sure the temperature can be adjusted, depending on the time of year and the location.

4.5 Floor or chair

Ensure that participants will be comfortable and have enough space to sit or lie down, depending on what you decide. We prefer to seat participants on the floor or around a table because some people fall asleep as soon as they lie down, missing the full experience, and may even snore, disturbing others.

But feel free to arrange the space as you see fit, considering you intention and the logistics for the celebration.

Ancestral ceremonies were typically held outdoors, hence the tradition of sitting on the ground/floor without chairs or cushions. Nowadays, we still like the idea of sitting on the ground, justifying it to stay connected to Mother Nature and to ground our root chakra (located at the base of the spine).

However, this is by no means essential. Life evolves, and we must adapt to the comforts available to us.

The key is to be comfortable and not get up with aches after sitting uncomfortably on the ground for several hours, as this can block the energy flow through your energy centers or chakras.

You decide what's best for you and your participants: floor or chair?

4.6 Basic comforts

One of the advantages of modern times is the availability of toilets. You no longer must go out into the field to take care of your needs, and at events where participants are encouraged to stay hydrated, accessible bathrooms are a must.

Make sure there are cushions, blankets, or any other items that may be needed. Once, we held a ceremony with chairs, and someone who was very short couldn't touch the ground with their feet, so we had to place a wooden fruit crate under their feet to help them "ground." It is important for participants to feel "anchored" to the earth during the ceremony.

Ceremony held indoors

Cacao preparation: Very Important! Where are you going to cook the cacao? It may be convenient to buy a portable stove with gas cartridges or an electric cable so that you can perform the cacao preparation ritual wherever you want without limitations. Consider this, as they take up little space and are relatively inexpensive!

But it is also possible to cook the cacao beforehand in another site and bring it to the ceremony in a thermal flask to keep it warm.

In any case, we consider it essential to visit the ceremony venue a couple of days before to assess any potential challenges and address them. It is helpful to have a checklist covering all the important aspects, where you can note down your observations and needs.

CHAPTER 5

ENERGY CLEANSING

When it comes to conducting a cacao ceremony, preparing the space is essential to ensuring an appropriate atmosphere. If the celebration is held at your own venue, it is likely that you will already keep it clean both physically and energetically.

However, if you have been invited to hold the ceremony in someone else's home or venue, it is crucial that the space is physically clean before proceeding with the energetic cleansing.

First, ask the hosts to clean the place physically. We do not want to hurt anyone's feelings or be rude, but physical dirt can attract dense energies.

A good sweeping, scrubbing, and airing out are initial steps to raising the space's vibrational frequency, allowing the spirit of cacao to act more smoothly and effectively.

There are many methods to energetically cleanse a space, all of which are valid and effective. The key is the intention to cleanse and elevate the energy of the space.

There are numerous resources available, such as books, workshops, and information online, to help you find the technique that resonates most with you.

One of my teachers always said:

> **"If it's simple, it's spiritual; if it's complicated, it's ego."**

This means you should use the technique that is simplest and most accessible to you.

This book does not focus on energetic cleansing techniques, but we will share our preferred method based on experience and affinity.

5.1 Cleansing with minerals&essential oils

We prepare two sprays for energetic cleansing:

A. Energetic cleansing spray (for half a liter of water):

- A glass or plastic spray bottle.
- Spring or bottled water.
- A polished black tourmaline that fits through the spray bottle's opening.
- 10 drops of lemon essential oil.
- 10 drops of lavender essential oil.

B. Harmonizing spray (for half a liter of water):

- A glass or plastic spray bottle.
- Spring or bottled water.
- A transparent quartz that fits through the spray bottle's opening.
- 4 drops of rose essential oil or the equivalent of 100 ml of rose water or orange blossom water.

Spray dispensers

The preparation process is quite simple. You just need to follow these steps:

1. Gather all the necessary ingredients according to the recipe or preparation you wish to make.
2. Place all the ingredients in a suitable bottle or container. Ensure the container is clean and dry before adding the ingredients.
3. Let the ingredients blend in the bottle for 6 hours. During this time, the energy of the ingredients will transfer to the water.

This process allows the elements to release their properties and benefits into the water, creating a mixture that can be used according to your needs.

Using the cleansing spray (A), spray the corners and center of the space while invoking the archangels, repeating the following phrase at least three times:

> *"I invoke Archangel Michael to cleanse and purify this space from negative energies and low densities."*

Then, use the harmonizing spray (B) and repeat in the corners and center of the space, saying:

> *"I invoke Archangel Michael to protect this space, Archangel Gabriel to harmonize this space, Archangel Chamuel to fill this space with love and respect, Archangel Raphael to fill this space with healing, prosperity, and abundance, and Archangel Jophiel to fill this space with wisdom and inspiration."*

Finally, use the tuning forks from the angelic kit, whose high frequency helps "dissolve" negative energies and seal the space.

Once you feel the space is cleansed of low-density energies, proceed to the phase of raising the vibrational frequency culminating in the creation of the altar or "Tlamanalli". This altar will maintain the vibration of the space elevated during the ceremony.

5.2 Maintaining a sacred environment

When the ceremony takes place outdoors in a natural environment, fewer precautions are needed compared to an indoor space, such as a house, educational center, or convention hall, as nature itself cleanses and transmutes low-density energies.

However, when the celebration is held indoors, it is important to maintain the purity and connection with the sacred environment.

To achieve this, we recommend that participants leave their shoes and mobile devices outside the ceremony room.

This practice not only helps preserve the cleanliness of the space but also symbolizes the entrance to a state of presence and reverence. Disconnecting from the distractions of the outside world allows for a greater space of connection and awareness.

5.3 Facilitator preparation

Physical preparation

A celebration is always an act of joy and gratitude, and it is essential to flow with that energy. However, on the day of the celebration, unforeseen events may occur that unsettle, anger, or worry you.

In these moments, it is crucial to rely on energetic techniques to keep your vibration high.

We recommend that a few hours before the event you take a 20–40-minute walk in nature. If you live in the city, find the nearest park. Trees and vegetation have the mission of balancing us, and the green of nature calms our heart chakra.

Afterward, take a bath or shower, scrubbing your entire body with coarse salt. This will help you remove dead skin and clear any accumulated negative energy from your aura.

Dress in white, as this color contains all colors and will help you connect with higher planes and feel inspired. Adorn yourself with necklaces, bracelets, and earrings that make you feel good, preferably made of natural fabrics.

We recommend wearing rose quartz, amethyst, clear quartz bracelets, and a protective symbol, such as a bracelet or pendant made of obsidian, tourmaline, jet, or black onyx.

Black minerals are excellent for protecting your auric field and keeping you centered during the celebration.

Avoid using perfumes, and make sure your deodorant is not too strong, as some people may be allergic to certain chemicals, which could cause discomfort during the celebration.

Spiritual and energetic preparation of the facilitator

This ceremony allows us to deeply connect with ourselves and the spirit of cacao. Through this practice, we can open our hearts and receive the teachings and healing energy of this sacred plant.

As a facilitator, you must prepare yourself properly before the event by following these steps:

- Take a moment to sit quietly with the cacao you will prepare in your hands.
- Close your eyes and breathe deeply, feeling the aroma and energy of the cacao.
- Visualize a golden light emanating from the cacao, surrounding you and filling you with love and warmth.
- Speak to the spirit of cacao from your heart, thanking for its presence and asking for its guidance and wisdom during the ceremony.

Of course, you can adapt this invocation as you see fit; the important thing is to connect with the cacao and ask for its blessing and guidance.

Before the participants arrive, take a few minutes to sit in a chair, resting your back comfortably, without crossing your legs, and with your feet firmly on the ground.

Close your eyes, take a deep breath, and ask your guardian angel, guide, or any being you connect with for guidance, so the celebration serves the highest good for everyone.

This simple preparation will raise your frequency and allow everything to flow with ease and love.

CAPITULO 6

CEREMONIAL CACAO RECIPE

There is no single recipe for ceremonial cacao. The only essential ingredient is cacao, and the choice of the type of cacao depends on the facilitator's taste and the availability of varieties in your region.

Below is a general guide for preparing one liter of ceremonial cacao drink.

Remember that these proportions and steps are just a guide. You can adjust the quantities and ingredients according to the preferences of the participants and the availability of ingredients. The key is to maintain the spirit of the ceremony and respect the essence of cacao.

The amount of drink to prepare depends on the number of participants. As a general guide, calculate about 150 ml per person, including yourself. This will ensure that each participant has enough to fully enjoy the ceremony.

Proportions for one liter of ceremonial cacao drink

Here are the approximate proportions for preparing one liter of ceremonial cacao drink:

- **Pure cacao**: Between 25-50 g per person. The usual amount is about 35 g for 200 ml so you would need 175 grmsl
- **Water**: 1000 ml
- **Sweetener**: To taste
- **Spices:** To taste

6.1 Liquid base

You need a liquid base in which to dissolve or emulsify the cacao.

We choose to prepare the drink traditionally with water rather than cow's milk. Although milk may taste better to some, people can be allergic to elements like casein and lactose, and we want to avoid any discomfort during the ceremony.

But "water" can also be prepared in several ways, and here are some examples to inspire you to create many more:

Bottled water base: The more natural the water—without chlorine, heavy metals, or minerals—the better it is for health and the taste of the drink.

Rose water base: Infuse 5 g of rose petals in a liter of water until the water turns pink.

Chai tea base: Chai tea is a blend of plants used in infusions, and each brand has its own formula, though most contain green tea, cinnamon, cardamom, ginger, clove, black pepper, and nutmeg. Use one bag of your preferred chai tea in a liter of water.

Mint base: Use a mint tea bag in a liter of water. This brings a flavor reminiscent of those classic English chocolates with a hint of creamy mint—perfect for a refreshing touch!

Plant-based base: You can choose from almond, soy, rice, oat, millet, or walnut plant-based drinks.

If you are looking for a gentler option that's less likely to cause allergies, we recommend rice milk, as it has a neutral flavor and will still taste delicious.

Your own favorite base: Infuse a liter of water with ingredients that resonate with you and that you genuinely enjoy. Do not make a base thinking of others' preferences if it's not something you love!

6.2 Ceremonial cacao ingredients

Our recommendation is to use few ingredients and in small quantities.

Human taste is highly varied, and what one person likes, another might dislike. Since we do not know the preferences of all the participants, the simpler the recipe, the more likely it will appeal to a larger number of people.

You can also change the base of the drink according to the season. In warmer times, something light is more appealing, such as a base with citrus (orange peel, grapefruit, tangerine, etc.).

In colder seasons, you can opt for richer and spicier flavors, like cinnamon, cardamom, pepper, etc.

Have fun creating your own formulas and testing which ones your audience enjoys the most. Tastes vary from country to country and culture to culture, so adapt your recipe wherever you go!

A warm cup of ceremonial cacao

We always use a base of rose petals and, depending on the season or the country we are in, we add one or more of the following ingredients per liter of water:

QUANTITY	INGREDIENT
5 grams	Rose petals: Preferably Castilian rose as its flower is small and very fragrant.
1 square cm	Natural ginger with skin.
3 cm of stick	Cinnamon.
5 cm of pod	Vanilla or 5 to 6 drops of vanilla extract.
10 cm	Citrus peel (orange, lime, lemon).
5 berries	Black peppercorns.

This process requires two steps:

1. **Rose petal infusion:** Place the petals in an infusion bag and put them in the pot with lukewarm water for a couple of minutes until the water turns pink, indicating that the flowers have infused the water with their energy. After this time, remove the bag, and the base liquid is ready.
2. **Infusion of other ingredients:** Heat the rose water in the pot where you will prepare the cacao drink without boiling it. Once heated, introduce another infusion bag with the rest of the ingredients and let it steep for about 5 minutes. Remove the bag once the time has passed.

Once the infusion is ready, add the cacao and start stirring with a wooden, stainless-steel spoon, or a cacao whisk. The cooking process for the cacao lasts between 5 and 10 minutes, depending on the type of cacao you are using. Experience will tell you when your ceremonial cacao is ready.

Add the cacao: Add 175 grams of pure cacao to the hot water. Stir constantly with a spoon to ensure the cacao dissolves completely and there are no lumps.

Incorporate the sweetener: If you decide to sweeten the drink, add the natural sweetener of your choice. The amount will depend on your personal preference, but we suggest not making it too sweet. The cacao flavor should not be masked.

Stir and heat: Continue stirring the mixture while it heats. Be sure to keep the temperature steady without boiling. The goal is to keep the drink warm and homogeneous.

Serve: Once the cacao is fully dissolved and the mixture looks uniform, serve the drink in cups. Make sure each participant receives approximately 150 ml, with the option of having more if they wish.

Preparing the ceremonial cacao drink is a personal and adaptable process.

The key is to use high-quality pure cacao and adjust the proportions based on the number of participants.

By following these basic instructions and experimenting with different sweeteners and spices, you can create a unique drink that enriches the cacao ceremony experience for all participants.

Some facilitators prefer not to use a rose water infusion and, instead, add dried rose petals or small buds directly into each cup of cacao. This practice aims to promote heart-opening, as roses are known for fostering love energy.

We do not share this practice because, although roses are edible, the experience of finding something unexpected and with an uncomfortable texture while drinking cacao can be unpleasant. The instinct to spit out something unexpected in a drink is natural, as our body tends to react defensively to hard or scratchy objects in food and drinks that are generally smooth.

Before performing the ceremony, it is advisable to practice preparing the drink to become familiar with the process and adjust the proportions according to your personal preferences.

6.3 Sweeteners

Just as there are people who do not add sugar to their coffee or teas, many people also choose not to sweeten their cacao. So, it is possible you may attend a ceremony and find the drink quite bitter.

Cacao, with its deep and slightly bitter flavor, is a perfect base for experimenting with natural sweeteners. Each of these sweeteners not only add sweetness but also a unique flavor profile and beneficial nutritional properties.

Below, we explore some of the most popular natural sweeteners that can be added to cacao, describing their characteristics and how they affect the flavor of this delicious food, arranged by glycemic index and noting which are suitable for diabetics.

Sweeteners

We like to add a bit of sweetener, but without turning it into a syrup.In keeping with what is most natural and healthy, we use one of these sweeteners depending on the occasion and where we are.

STEVIA	
Glycemic Index	0
Flavor & Characteristics	Stevia is a natural sweetener derived from the leaves of the Stevia rebaudiana plant. It is much sweeter than sugar, so only a very small amount is needed.
Properties	Calorie-free and does not affect blood sugar levels, making it suitable for people with diabetes or those reducing calorie intake.
Taste with Cacao	May have a slightly bitter or licorice-like aftertaste; works well with cacao in small amounts.
Suitable for Diabetics	Yes

XYLITOL	
Glycemic Index	7
Flavor & Characteristics	A sugar alcohol found naturally in many fruits and vegetables. Taste very similar to sugar, with fewer calories.
Properties	Very low glycemic index and does not cause blood sugar spikes. Supports dental health by reducing the risk of cavities.
Taste with Cacao	Provides a clean, fresh sweetness similar to regular sugar without extra calories.
Suitable for Diabetics	Yes

AGAVE NECTAR	
Glycemic Index	15–30
Flavor & Characteristics	Extracted from the agave plant. Sweeter than sugar, honey-like texture with a neutral, slightly fruity flavor.
Properties	Low glycemic index; suitable for blood sugar control but use in moderation due to high fructose content.
Taste with Cacao	Adds a soft, delicate sweetness without significantly altering cacao's natural flavor.
Suitable for Diabetics	Yes, in moderation

COCONUT SUGAR

Glycemic Index	35
Flavor & Characteristics	Made from the sap of coconut palm flowers. Similar to brown sugar with caramel and slight nutty notes.
Properties	Lower glycemic index than refined sugar; contains minerals like iron, zinc, and potassium.
Taste with Cacao	Enhances cacao with caramel and nutty notes, adding depth and richness.
Suitable for Diabetics	Yes, in moderation

PANELA

Glycemic Index	55
Flavor & Characteristics	Unrefined sweetener from sugarcane juice with a strong caramel flavor and dark color.
Properties	Retains nutrients such as calcium, iron, and magnesium; a more natural alternative to refined sugar.
Taste with Cacao	Adds a robust caramelized flavor that complements cacao's bitterness.
Suitable for Diabetics	Not recommended

MAPLE SYRUP	
Glycemic Index	54
Flavor & Characteristics	Made from maple tree sap. Distinctive, robust flavor with caramel and woody notes.
Properties	Good source of antioxidants and minerals like manganese and zinc; moderate glycemic index.
Taste with Cacao	Adds a rich, complex sweetness with a slightly smoky touch.
Suitable for Diabetics	Not recommended

HONEY	
Glycemic Index	58
Flavor & Characteristics	Natural sweetener produced by bees from flower nectar; flavor varies by floral source, generally sweet with floral and light caramel notes.
Properties	Rich in antioxidants, vitamins, and minerals; antibacterial and anti-inflammatory; contains enzymes that support digestion.
Taste with Cacao	Adds a complex floral sweetness, balancing cacao's bitterness and giving a smooth texture.
Suitable for Diabetics	Not recommended

Experimenting with these sweeteners can transform a simple cup of cocoa into a rich and delicious experience, full of nutritional benefits and exceptional taste.

6.4 Preparing the cacao

There are different approaches to preparing cacao before a ceremony. Some facilitators prefer to cook the cacao in advance and reheat it just before the event, serving it in the same pot it was cooked in or transferring it to a more suitable container for the ceremony.

Others, due to venue limitations, opt to prepare the cacao beforehand and keep it warm in a thermos flask.

We, whenever possible, prefer to prepare the cacao as part of the ceremony, in front of the participants.

We believe the cacao begins to work its magic as it is being prepared, and involving the attendees in its preparation creates a deeper connection with the ritual.

We like to blend the ancient with the modern to get the best of both worlds. For example, while air conditioning or fans did not exist in the past, it doesn't mean we shouldn't use them if it gets hot during the ceremony.

Make the most of every moment and situation to offer a comfortable and meaningful experience.

Preparing ceremonial cacao

6.5 Equipment

There are many utensils that can be used to prepare cacao, and we like to choose those that combine aesthetics and comfort.

Transparent container
We prefer to prepare cacao in a transparent pot as it allows us to see how the water turns pink when the filter with rose petals is added. We find this method cleaner and more aesthetically pleasing, providing an attractive visual experience for the participants.

To stir the mixture, we use either a wooden spoon or a stainless-steel one. At the end of the process, we use a traditional Mexican "molinillo", specifically designed to create foam in the cacao, resulting in a creamy texture that enhances both the presentation and the experience when serving the cacao in cups. However, feel free to use any utensil of your choice, such as a stainless-steel whisk.

Glass ladle

To pour the cacao into individual containers, we use a glass ladle that matches our pot. You can use whatever you find most suitable.

Cups

Individual containers can be made of clay, earthenware, glass, wood, metal, or any other material, but avoid plastic whenever possible due to its toxic content and low vibrational frequency.

We recommend small cups, around 150 ml, as some people may find the flavor or texture of cacao too intense and may feel uncomfortable if they can't finish it.

Even if they only take a few sips, the spirit of the cacao enters their body and does its magic. You can be sure of that!

6.6 Amount of cacao to consume

Participants may have as much as they like, but we recommend limiting the intake to 200 ml per serving. Sacred plants should be consumed in moderation. It is different from eating a piece of chocolate, where the cacao concentration is lower, compared to drinking pure cacao. A little is medicine; too much can lead to indigestion.

6.7 Tips for preparation and transportation

It is possible that you'll be able to use the utensils available at the venue, but over time, you'll realize that you prefer using your own. We organize ceremonies for up to 22 people.

If we travel to another location, we bring a suitcase with the essentials for the ceremony: the portable stove, cacao "molinillo," pot, individual containers, ladle, ingredients for the cacao beverage, and cherished items for the altar. Other elements, such as candles, incense, flowers, and pens, are purchased at destination.

Preparing ceremonial cacao requires attention to detail and a mix of traditional and modern methods. Use suitable utensils and involve the participants in the process, adapting your practices to the venue conditions. This will ensure a meaningful and enjoyable experience for everyone involved.

CHAPTER 7

MEDICINE MUSIC FOR CACAO CEREMONIES

Music is a powerful tool in cacao ceremonies, acting as a bridge between the physical and the spiritual. A carefully curated playlist can transform a simple gathering into a deeply healing and connective experience.

Throughout cacao ceremonies, melodies and chants not only create a sacred atmosphere but also facilitate emotional openness and introspection. In this context, a well-crafted playlist is essential to support the ceremony's intention and flow, ensuring that each moment is an opportunity for healing and profound connection.

In this chapter, we will provide you with the basic knowledge to help you use music and instruments so that your celebration is as enriching as possible.

You will learn how to select the right songs, use various instruments to enhance experience, and create an environment that promotes heart opening and connection among the participants.

7.1 Origin of medicine music

Music has been an integral part of ceremonies and rituals since ancient times. In ancient Mesoamerican civilizations, music was not only a form of entertainment but also a tool for healing and spiritual connection.

Drums, flutes, and chants were part of religious and healing ceremonies, used to invoke the gods, ask for good harvests, and heal illnesses.

"Medicine music" is a modern term that encompasses these ancestral practices, referring to melodies and chants created specifically to promote healing, meditation, and connection with the spirit.

This music has deep roots in indigenous and shamanic traditions, and its purpose is to harmonize body, mind, and spirit, creating a sacred space for personal transformation.

7.2 The healing vibrations of music

Science has begun to explore and validate what ancient traditions already knew: music has a profound impact on the brain and body.

Numerous studies have shown that listening to music can reduce levels of cortisol, the stress hormone, and increase the production of dopamine and endorphins, neurotransmitters associated with pleasure and happiness.

Music can influence brain waves, leading the listener into deep states of meditation and relaxation. From a spiritual and energetic perspective, music is considered a vibration that can elevate our energetic frequency.

Different types of music can activate and balance the chakras, the body's energy centers, facilitating greater internal harmony and a deeper connection with the universe.

7.3 The power of chanting and spoken words

Chants, especially in a ceremonial context, have the power to transform our mood and biochemistry. Repetitive chants and mantras can induce trance-like states and deep meditation, facilitating the release of emotional and physical tensions.

Group chanting creates collective resonance, unifying individual energies into harmonious vibration. This practice can strengthen the sense of community and connection among participants, creating a safe and sacred space for personal and collective transformation.

In addition to chanting, spoken words also have immense power to influence our mind and body. The way we speak and the words we choose can significantly affect our emotional and physical state.

Positive affirmations and words of encouragement can elevate our mood, reduce stress, and promote overall well-being. In a ceremonial context, spoken word becomes a sacred tool that guides the group's energy and sets the intention for the ceremony.

Spoken words, like chanting, produces vibrations that resonate in our body and mind. These vibrations can activate and balance the chakras, promoting internal harmony. In cacao ceremonies, words and chants are used to invoke healing and spiritual connection.

The resonance of these vibrations can facilitate the release of emotional and energetic blockages, allowing energy to flow freely and promoting healing.

7.4 Lullabies and medicine music

Lullabies, or soothing songs for babies, are known for their ability to calm and provide security with their gentle and repetitive melodies. Similarly, the medicine music used in cacao ceremonies has a calming and healing effect on participants.

These melodies, like lullabies, create an atmosphere of tranquility and love, providing a safe emotional foundation and fostering heart-opening.

In cacao ceremonies, medicine music acts as a balm for the soul, helping participants relax, release tension, and connect deeply with their emotions.

7.5 The power of humming

The simple act of humming can have significant effects on our mental and emotional health. This seemingly simple action can induce a state of calm and focus.

Humming creates an internal vibration that gently massages the inner structures of the ear and brain, promoting a sense of well-being. In cacao ceremonies, humming is used to center the mind and open the heart, facilitating a deeper connection with oneself and with other participants.

Humming can be a form of sound meditation, helping to release tension and balance emotions. Additionally, it is an accessible practice for everyone, requiring no musical skills, allowing anyone to participate and benefit from its healing effects.

7.6 Key songs and voices in cacao rituals

In cacao ceremonies, certain songs have gained popularity for their ability to elevate the spirit and create a sacred atmosphere. Each song is a tool to guide participants on their inner journey, facilitating introspection and healing.

These songs have their own melody and special meaning, such as:

> ***Madre Tierra by Isis Montemayor*** – Celebrates the connection with nature and Mother Earth.

Los cuatro elementos by Pedro Vadhar – Honors the spirit of the four elements.

Cacao abre el corazón by Boveda Celeste – Pays homage to the power of cacao as a source of connection with joy and the heart.

Cacaosito la medicina by Karunika – Invocation for healing through cacao.

En espiral hacia dentro by Ivan Donalson – An ode to the Tlamanalli.

These songs not only enhance the ceremony but also help participants enter a state of meditation and deep connection.

The richness of Mesoamerican music is reflected in the work of various authors and musicians who have kept the tradition of ceremonial chants alive.

Artists like Jorge Reyes, with his fusion of pre-Hispanic and modern sounds, and Tito La Rosa, with his interpretations of traditional Andean music, are just a few examples of artists who have contributed to the preservation and dissemination of medicine music.

Jorge Reyes is known for his innovative use of pre-Hispanic and electronic instruments to create soundscapes that evoke ancient rituals. Tito La Rosa, on the other hand, is a master of the Andean flute and uses his music to heal and connect people with their spiritual roots.

Their works are a bridge between the past and the present, offering new generations a way to connect with their cultural and spiritual roots.

Other contemporary artists like Lila Downs, Natalia Lafourcade, Bruno Mansur, Mose, Ayla Schafer, Danit, and Mose have also explored and revitalized Mesoamerican musical traditions in their works, bringing these ancient melodies to a global audience.

For ceremonies, it is essential to have a varied repertoire that includes both songs and instrumental melodies. At times, the lyrics of songs can interrupt participants' concentration and reflection, so it is advisable to opt for instrumental music that serves as a soft and immersive background.

It is crucial to identify the right moments for each type of music. During phases of meditation, introspection, or activities that require deep focus, instrumental or ambient music is ideal because it creates a tranquil atmosphere and facilitates inner connection.

On the other hand, there are moments in the ceremony when songs with lyrics can enrich the experience. These songs can resonate with the theme of the ceremony, bring a sense of unity, and uplift the participants' spirits.

The lyrics can support and enhance the activities being carried out, providing an emotional and meaningful context that strengthens the event's intention.

7.7 How to find medicine music

Due to the growing popularity of cacao ceremonies, it is quite easy to find suitable music for your celebrations. Below are some recommended sources:

1. Spotify: This platform offers a wide variety of playlists specific to cacao ceremonies. You can search for terms like "Cacao Ceremony," "Shamanic Music," "Medicine Music" or "Healing Music" to find specialized lists that suit the atmosphere you want to create.

2. YouTube: On YouTube, you can find channels dedicated to ceremonial and spiritual music. Some of the most popular include:

3. Medicina Sonora: A channel with music specifically for cacao ceremonies and other spiritual practices.

4. Shaman's Dream Music: Music created especially for ceremonies, meditations, and healing.

5. Liquid Bloom: Musical projects that combine electronic sounds with ceremonial and ethnic elements.

6. SoundCloud: Many independent artists upload their music to SoundCloud, where you can find tracks and playlists ideal for cacao ceremonies. Search tags like "Cacao Ceremony," "Ambient," "Shamanic," "Ayahuasca" "Icaros" and "Healing."

7. Bandcamp: This platform allows independent artists to sell their music directly to listeners. You can find full albums dedicated to ceremonial music, often with the option to listen before purchasing.

8. Meditation Apps: Apps like Calm, Insight Timer, and Headspace offer guided meditations, as well as music and ambient sounds that can be perfect for cacao ceremonies.

9. Specialized Websites: There are websites dedicated to music for ceremonies and spiritual events.

10. Sacred cacao ceremony music: Websites offering downloads o music specially created for cacao ceremonies.

11. Sound healing academy: Providers of healing music that can be used in your ceremonies.

These sources will provide you with a wide range of options to choose the perfect music that will enrich and complement you cacao ceremonies, creating an atmosphere conducive to introspection and spiritual connection.

Scan this QR to access a Spotify playlist with the songs we mos often use in our cacao ceremonies, along with a collection of hand picked resources to support and inspire your own practice Everything is right here, easy to access whenever you need it.

You can also access it from:

https://thewingbook.com/en/bonus/cacao-ceremony/

7.8 Rituals and healing chants

Healing chants are used in a variety of rituals and celebrations, each with their own purpose and cultural context. Some of the most well-known include:

Cacao celebrations:

In this celebration, chants are used to open the heart and connect participants with the spirit of cacao. The songs create a sacred atmosphere, facilitating meditation, introspection, and connection with others.

Chants are often accompanied by instruments the facilitator feels comfortable with, adding a rhythmic dimension to the experience. In cacao ceremonies, music plays a fundamental role in creating a space for healing and personal transformation.

Ayahuasca ceremonies:

Ayahuasca is a sacred plant used in shamanic ceremonies in the Amazon. During these ceremonies, shamans or facilitators sing "icaros", sacred chants that guide participants through their inner journey. These chants help purify the body and spirit and invoke the protection of the jungle spirits.

Temazcal ceremonies:

A "temazcal" is a traditional Mesoamerican steam bath used for physical and spiritual purification. During the ceremony, sacred chants are sung to invoke the four elements and ancestral spirits. The chants help participants release toxins and renew their energy.

Healing drum rituals:

In many Indigenous cultures, the drum is considered a sacred instrument that connects the physical and spiritual worlds.

During these rituals, specific rhythms are played, and healing chants are sung to invoke the assistance of spirits and harmonize the body and mind.

Peyote ceremonies:

Peyote is a cactus used by native people in northern Mexico and the southwestern United States. Peyote ceremonies include chants that guide and protect participants during their visionary journey.

These chants, accompanied by the rhythm of the drum, are considered essential for healing and spiritual connection.

Meditations and chanting circles:

In more contemporary settings, chanting circles and guided meditations with music also use healing chants. These gatherings provide a safe space for self-exploration and emotional healing, using music as a tool to deepen meditation and group connection.

7.9 Sing without being a professional

Many people may feel insecure about singing in public, especially in a ceremonial setting. However, you do not need to have a perfect voice or professional musical skills to participate in healing chants.

The purpose of these chants is connection and healing, not technical perfection.

If you are not comfortable singing, you can simply hum the melodies. As we have seen before, humming creates a gentle vibration that can be just as effective for meditation and spiritual connection.

Another option is to play recorded music and chants through good speakers. There are many high-quality recordings of ceremonial chants and healing music that can enrich the ceremony's experience.

7.10 Musical instruments you can play in a ceremony

In ceremonies, music plays a vital role in creating a sacred environment and facilitates spiritual connection.

Musical instruments not only add beauty to the ceremony, but they also help harmonize energies and guide meditations.

Here are some instruments you can play in a ceremony, each with its own character and purpose.

Tibetan bowls: Also known as singing bowls, these instruments produce deep sounds and vibrations that can induce states of meditation and relaxation. Tibetan bowls are used to balance chakras and energetically cleanse the ceremonial space.

Crystal bowls: Made from pure quartz, these bowls produce clear and resonant sounds.

They are particularly effective for healing and deep meditation, used to amplify energy and raise the vibrational frequency of the participants.

Some instruments used in ceremonies

Rainstick: This instrument, also known as a rainstick, produces a relaxing sound that resembles the falling of water. It is used to bring tranquility and peace to the ceremonial environment, helping participants connect with nature and their inner self.

Shamanic drum: The drum is one of the oldest and most sacred instruments. Its deep, repetitive rhythms can induce trance states and facilitate shamanic journeying. It is used to invoke spirits and anchor energy during the ceremony.

Maracas: Maracas produce a rhythmic sound that helps maintain the beat and energize the ceremonial space. They are ideal for accompanying chants and adding an element of joy and movement to the ceremony.

Native american flute: The flute produces melodic and ethereal sounds that can transport listeners to a state of peace and contemplation. It is used to connect with the spirits of nature and to guide meditation.

Tibetan bells (tingshas): These bells produce a clear, resonant sound used to energetically cleanse the space and mark the beginning and end of meditations and ceremonies.

Kalimba: Also known as a thumb piano, the kalimba produces a sweet and melodic sound. It is used to create a relaxing atmosphere and to accompany chants and meditations.

Didgeridoo: This wind instrument of Aboriginal Australian origin produces a deep and vibrant sound that can induce trance and meditation states. It is used for healing and to connect with the earth and its energies.

Guitar and variations: The guitar, ukulele, and other guitar variations are extremely versatile and popular in ceremonies. Their ability to accompany chants and create enveloping melodies makes them an excellent choice for almost any type of ceremony.

Handpan: This melodic percussion instrument produces harmonic and relaxing sounds. It is ideal for creating a meditative atmosphere and guiding participants into deep introspection.

Harp: The harp produces an ethereal and celestial sound that can elevate the ceremonial atmosphere to a higher spiritual level. This instrument is associated with angels and is used to accompany chants and create a soft, harmonious musical background.

Shruti box: This Indian-origin instrument produces a continuous and harmonic sound used to accompany chants and mantras. It is ideal for maintaining constant vibration and supporting meditation.

Gong: The gong produces a powerful and resonant sound that can cleanse and transform the energy of the ceremonial space. It is used to open and close ceremonies and to induce deep meditation states.

These instruments, each with their own qualities and effects, can be used in ceremonies to create a sacred space, harmonize energies, and guide participants on their inner journey.

Whether you are an experienced musician or a beginner, the most important thing is to play with intention and from the heart, allowing the music to flow and elevate the ceremonial experience.

We recommend that you delve deeper into the songs and musical instruments, as they form a fundamental part of any ceremony and will be of great use to you.

CHAPTER 8

TLAMANALLI: THE CEREMONIAL ALTAR

In any ritual or ceremony, there is a sacred space intended to connect with higher beings and fulfill functions related to spiritual planes. In our cacao celebration, we follow the rich traditions of the Mexican people preserved through their Nahuatl language. This sacred space is called the Tlamanalli.

8.1 Origin and meaning of the Tlamanalli

The word Tlamanalli comes from the Nahuatl term that translates to "offering to the earth." It derives from *tlamana*, meaning "earth," and the suffix *-lli*, meaning "the offering." It reflects the worldview of the Nahuatl people, becoming the point of connection with the sacred.

The Tlamanalli has its roots in the traditional knowledge of Nahuatl women. This knowledge includes aspects such as traditional medicine, natural resources' management, agriculture, and reproductive health, all linked to spirituality and nature.

Women, who have the power to transmit life, are traditionally responsible for preparing the Tlamanalli. They trace the four cardinal points on the altar, starting in the East and following the course of the sun to infuse energy into the entire environment.

This traditional and ancestral knowledge, which forms the cultural base, is passed down to their sons and daughters through the bloodline and daily teachings of indigenous women.

For the Nahuatl people, nature is alive and sacred because its elements—rivers, forests, animals, stones, mountains—are considered gods, spirits, or allies.

In the Tlamanalli, the four elements—earth, fire, water, and air—are represented through various objects.

The Tlamanalli is more than just an altar; it is the heart of the cacao ceremony. Its arrangement and the elements that compose it create a sacred circle that connects participants with the divine and enhances ancestral wisdom.

This space helps elevate the vibrational frequency of the place, ensuring that the ceremony unfolds in an atmosphere of high energy and spiritual connection.

Through the Tlamanalli, we honor the wisdom and traditions of Indigenous peoples, creating a bridge between the visible and the invisible, the earthly and the divine, allowing the energy of cacao to flow with greater intensity and purpose.

The Tlamanalli also acts as a catalyst for healing and inner rebirth. By following its rhythms and cycles, participants can release old patterns, receive inspiration, and nurture their spiritual and personal growth.

8.2 Symbolism of an altar or Tlamanalli

In any celebration or ritual, a specific area is always reserved in the venue where the event will unfold to position objects that connect us with other dimensions and bring us closer to our essence, the Universe, and God.

Depending on the nature of the ceremony, different objects are used to help facilitate the connection sought with other planes.

Following the most practiced ancestral traditions, the Tlamanalli is a circle divided into four parts, where each section has its representative elements. It is recommended to start with the four directions, their elements, and associated colors.

The relationship between the elements and the four cardinal points is based on various spiritual and shamanic traditions, where each cardinal direction is associated with one of the four natural elements (air, fire, water, and earth) and their corresponding qualities.

This relationship between elements and cardinal points is based on various spiritual and shamanic traditions, where each cardinal direction is associated with one of the four natural elements (air, fire, water and earth) and their corresponding qualities.

This relationship between the elements and the cardinal directions can vary slightly between different cultures and shamanic traditions, but the general principles are fairly universal. Here is the most commonly accepted explanation:

East – Air – White or yellow

> *Characteristics:* The East is the direction of dawn and new beginnings. Air symbolizes the breath of life, the mind, communication, and mental clarity. It is the place of spirit and inspiration. Totem Animals: Eagle, hawk.

South – Fire – Red

Characteristics: The South represents midday and the warmth of the sun. Fire is the symbol for energy, passion, creativity, and transformation. It is the direction of growth, strength, and action. Totem Animals: Jaguar, snake.

West – Water – Blue

Characteristics: The West is associated with dusk and mystery. Water represents emotions, intuition, healing, and renewal. It is the direction of introspection, the subconscious, and emotional cleansing. Totem Animals: Bear, salmon.

North – Earth – Black

Characteristics: The North is related to night and ancestral wisdom. Earth symbolizes stability, strength, knowledge, and protection. It is the direction of harvest, maturity, and connection with the physical. Totem Animals: Buffalo, deer.

Center (Heart of the Circle) Often considered spirit or ether

characteristics: The center symbolizes the union of all elements and directions. It represents the "here and now", balance, integrity, and connection with the divine.

The primary function of this altar is to provide a completely safe ceremony for the Facilitator and their guests, as the objects integrated into it are designed to absorb the dense energies that arise during a ceremony, preventing them from being taken by another member of the ceremony or even by the Facilitator.

This type of altar or offering must be made from the heart. Its design, despite existing traditions, depends entirely on the intention, materials, taste, and feelings the Facilitator has before creating the altar.

Fresh flowers should always be used due to their great capacity for absorption and retention. This means that as they wilt, the energy they have absorbed dissipates as well and can return to the earth, transmuting and preventing anyone else from absorbing what was released during the ceremony.

The objects selected to be included in the Tlamanalli should be related to the facilitator's intention and the purpose of the celebration to enhance the event.

The Tlamanalli is placed at the center of the celebration and is untouchable, acting as a sacred altar that cannot be crossed. To maintain its integrity, a circle is drawn around the Tlamanalli, creating a space where participants can be and move without disturbing the altar.

This circle represents an endless space that rises from the earth and spirals upward to the sky. As the oral tradition says, "We are a circle within a circle, with no beginning and no end."

Place a significant figure or element, such as a cacao fruit or a crystal quartz, in the center of the altar. Surround it with flowers, fruits, minerals, figures, and other elements.

If you want to follow the Nahuatl tradition, you can draw a cross or an X with four entrances, representing the four elements and cardinal points, and arrange the colors, elements, and flowers accordingly.

You can arrange the Tlamanalli in any harmonious design that resonates with your spiritual beliefs. On the internet and on our website, you will find examples of completed Tlamanallis. Do not copy them—use them only as inspiration.

Remember, your connection and creativity in choosing the elements and designing your Tlamanalli is what will make it personal and unique. Be inspired, but always ensure that your designs are your own, unique, and original.

8.3 Creating the Tlamanalli

In ancient Tlamanalli, the first thing placed at the center was a pre-Hispanic figurine to which the ritual would be offered, and around it laid fruits, herbs, flowers, grains, and foods to offer to the corresponding deity.

Today, you can place any important element, or something related to the theme you will be working on, such as a crystal quartz, a big candle, an angel figure... and around it, flowers, leaves, sticks, fruits, and elements that Mother Nature gives us.

To keep this energetically bound, you can place oracle cards in an outside circle aligned with the theme of the celebration. These could be angel cards, cacao cards, fairy cards, totem cards, etc.

It is important to note that the placement of these elements follows the criteria of the person leading the ceremony. However, tradition indicates that the most common arrangement is to create an X or a cross with four equal entrances, called "doors," establishing the main elements: water, fire, earth, and air.

This position is called *nahui ollin teotl* and is known as the four energies in motion. This cross should be contained within the circle of oracle cards.

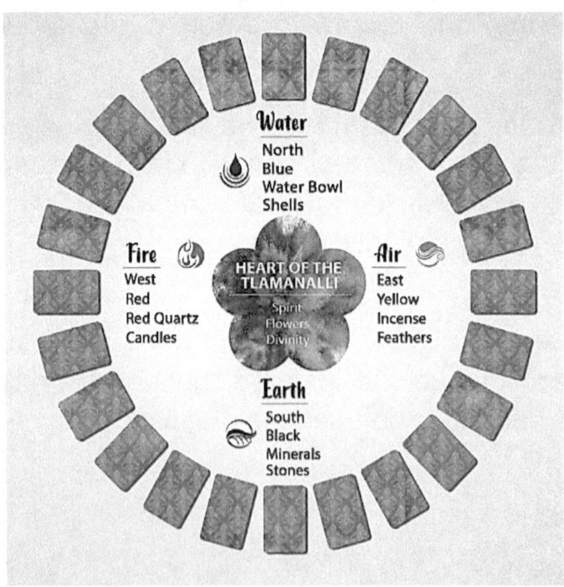

8.4 Materials for creating a Tlamanalli

You should have a variety of objects to use at any ceremony. These can be generic, whose properties are well known by most people involved in emotional or spiritual support, or personal objects that hold special meaning for you and bring comfort when performing heart-opening events.

Symmetry is something our brain appreciates, as one of its functions is to "file" things in different compartments. So, when you are creating your altar, keep this in mind and ensure you have enough of the same type of objects to achieve symmetry.

For example, if you are collecting small white stones, select those that are about the same size and color, and make sure to have at least fifty or more of them. It is better to have extra than to run out!

Use what nature provides depending on the season. In autumn/winter, it is easy to find diverse types of pinecones, walnuts, berries, etc .. Below you can find some inspiring objects:

ITEM	DESCRIPTION
Sea shells	Various types and sizes
Crystals	Tumbled stones, points or clusters of rose quartz, obsidians, agates, etc
Candles	Different sizes and colors
Stones	Different sizes and colors
Feathers	From various birds and sizes
Incense	Gentle scents that don't produce much smoke
Figurines	Representations of your guides, deities, etc
Oracle cards	Inspirational cards, not divinatory
Fruit	Apples, mandarins, oranges. Fruit seeds such as avocado, loquats, peach...
Nuts with shells	Pinecones, chestnuts, pecans, walnuts, hazelnuts, acorns

Flowers

Natural flowers are a "must" in all ceremonies to raise the frequency of the space. The color depends on your preference or the season since not all flowers are available year-round or in every country.

Don't cheat by using dried or fabric flowers, this won't help create the magical and high frequency atmosphere we're seeking for the ceremony.

It's tempting to pick and use beautiful wildflowers in spring, but I don't recommend it because their bloom doesn't last more than an hour once cut.

Choose flowers with large, vibrant petals whose color matches the theme of the event you are holding.

Flower selection and recommended colours

White: Always a safe choice, as it's the "wild card" color. Perfect for ceremonies with a more spiritual theme, representing purity, peace, and harmony.

Red: Ideal for ceremonies celebrating love, passion, or strength. Red flowers symbolize energy, vitality, and courage, perfect for empowerment and transformation rituals.

Yellow: Perfect for ceremonies aiming to attract joy, happiness, and prosperity. Yellow flowers represent sunlight, friendship, and creativity, suitable for optimistic and joyful celebrations.

Blue: Best for ceremonies seeking inner peace, serenity, and mental clarity. Blue flowers symbolize calm, wisdom, and communication, ideal for moments of reflection and spiritual connection.

Pink: Suitable for ceremonies related to unconditional love, compassion, and tenderness. Pink flowers represent softness, femininity, and affection, perfect for emotional healing and self-love rituals.

Purple: Ideal for ceremonies of transformation and connection with the spiritual realm. Purple flowers symbolize mystery, magic, and deep spirituality, suitable for introspection and personal growth rituals.

These recommendations can help you choose the most appropriate flowers for each type of ceremony, enhancing the intention and desired atmosphere.

When it comes to flowers, roses are found worldwide because they are strongly associated with the heart chakra and love, making them a great complement to altars.

However, many other flowers have powerful energy and are more affordable, making them a perfect choice for your Tlamanalli. Many will also be native to the area where you are holding your celebration.

Leaves and vegetation

Branches: Help define the areas of the Tlamanalli

Leaves: Their scent and decorative use are essential to completing the altar

8.5 Object arrangement in the Tlamanalli

Each Tlamanalli is a unique work of creation, and your inspiration will guide you in placing the different objects in their rightful place.

Let your intuition lead you, flowing with the energy of the moment. Allow your heart and spirit to connect with the elements and their deeper meanings.

Remember, there is no right or wrong way to arrange the objects. Each Tlamanalli reflects the unique intention and energy of the moment, as well as the individuals participating in the ceremony.

Tlamanalli with different ornaments

Consider the elements and their associations with the cardinal directions, along with any symbol or object that resonates with you and the purpose of the celebration.

Creativity and spiritual connection are your best allies in this process. Trust your ability to create a Tlamanalli that enhances the ceremony and honors the spirits and energies you invoke.

CHAPTER 9

CREATING THE RIGHT ATMOSPHERE

We've explored in-depth the essential elements that compose a cacao ceremony. Now, let's dive into the specific steps, from the participants' arrival to their departure.

9.1 Energetic cleansing of participants

Before entering the ceremonial space, it is essential to cleanse participants energetically.

This practice helps release any negative or stagnant energy, allowing each person to enter the ceremonial space with a higher vibration and an open heart.

Here are a few quick and non-invasive methods for performing this cleansing:

White sage

Burn a bundle of white sage and pass it around the participant's aura three times.

Sage is known for its purifying properties and can help clear unwanted energies. Be sure to use a bowl to collect the ashes and keep the space clean.

Tibetan bowl

The vibrant sound of a Tibetan bowl can deeply penetrate the participant's energy field, promoting harmony and cleansing. Pass the bowl around the participant's aura three times, allowing its vibrations to purify and balance.

Angel tunnng forks

Angel tuning forks emit healing frequencies that can cleanse and uplift the energy field. Activate them and pass them around the participant's aura three times to facilitate gentle and effective cleansing.

Once we have completed this preparatory work and followed the previous steps, it is time to begin the main part of the cacao ceremony.

Below is a chronological guide to the steps of a cacao ceremony. Some of the steps have been explained in-depth already, and others will be detailed later. You can always refer to the table of contents if you wish to skip to a specific section.

9.2. 9.2 Introducing the space

Most of the time, we do not mention certain things because they seem "obvious" to us, and we do not want to appear inconsequential.

However, what seems obvious to you may not be to someone else. That is why we recommend taking a few minutes at the beginning to share some logistical details, such as:

Location of the bathrooms: Clearly indicate where they are so participants feel comfortable.

Availability of cushions, blankets, etc.: Show them where they can find these items for their comfort during the ceremony.

A safe, judgment-free space: Reaffirm that this is a safe space, free from judgment, fostering an atmosphere of respect and acceptance.

Duration of the ceremony: Let participants know how long the ceremony will last so they can plan accordingly.

Structure of the ceremony: Briefly explain the ceremony's structure from start to finish, so participants know what to expect.

During these initial parts, it is recommended to play soft background music that doesn't interfere with the facilitator's voice. We suggest using instrumental music rather than songs with lyrics.

9.3 Introduction of the facilitator

Once the attendees are sitting around the Tlamanalli, it is important to make a small introduction about who you are and what brought you to facilitate these ceremonies.

People like to know something about the person in front of them. This is not about sharing your entire life story but revealing enough so they see you're a normal person, not a guru descended from the heavens.

You can follow these steps for your introduction:

Personal introduction:

State your name and a little about your background.

Explain how you discovered cacao ceremonies and what inspired you to facilitate them.

Experience and passion:

> Share some significant experiences you have had with Cacao.

> Talk about your passion for this practice and how it has impacted your life.

Purpose of the ceremony:

> Mention the purpose of the current ceremony and what you hope the participants will experience.

> Highlight that your goal is to create a safe and welcoming space for everyone.

Human connection:

> Emphasize that you are a human being with a story and personal journey, just like everyone else.

> Share a personal anecdote that resonates with the theme of the ceremony to establish a deeper connection with the attendees.

> By introducing yourself in this way, you help build an open, trusting relationship with the participants, creating a more intimate and authentic environment for the cacao ceremony.

9.4 Introduction of participants

It is also helpful for participants to introduce themselves. This helps build group cohesion. To make this activity enjoyable for everyone and avoid the nervousness that can come with speaking, you can turn the introductions into a game.

We usually do it in pairs, in the following way:

Each person is asked to pair up with the person to their right and decide who will be PERSON A and who will be PERSON B

For 30 seconds, Person A shares with Person B:
1. Their name

2. What they do for a living

3. What has brought them to the ceremony

After that time, PERSON B does the same with PERSON A.

Once the minute has passed and all pairs have finished, PERSON A seated to the right of the facilitator introduces their partner using the information they were given.

Then PERSON B does the same. This process continues until everyone has been introduced by their partner.

We use a small bell to mark the time, ensuring that all participants have the same amount of time for their introductions.

Introducing another person is usually easier and less intimidating than introducing oneself, and it helps create a more relaxed and welcoming atmosphere from the very beginning of the ceremony.

9.5 Unifying participants' energy

After the introductions, we move on to unifying the group's energy, as each person brings their own story, and we want the frequency to be high and flowing easily.

To do this, you'll guide participants through a brief meditation to calm the mind and open the heart.

This QR gives you access to a guided visualization to help you align with the energy of cacao, plus additional resources designed to support you in preparing and holding your own ceremonies.

You can also access it from:

https://thewingbook.com/en/bonus/cacao-ceremony/

CHAPTER 10
CEREMONY STEPS

10.1 Blessing and activation of the Tlamanalli

Once the introductions are done, it is time to begin the celebration, starting with the blessing and activation of the Tlamanalli by the facilitator. There is no single method for this, so we encourage you to use the one that resonates most with you and the energy present in the moment.

We usually begin by asking permission to: the four directions, Mother Earth, Father Sky, and the heart of cacao. This is the invocation we use:

East direction:

> We invoke the East, the direction of the sunrise and new beginnings. We call upon the spirits of air and wind, the energy of the eagle and hawk, to bring us clarity, vision, and wisdom. Welcome.

South direction

We invoke the South, the direction of midday and the warmth of the sun. We call upon the spirits of fire, the energy of the jaguar and the serpent, to bring us passion, transformation, and strength. Welcome.

West direction

We invoke the West, the direction of sunset and mystery. We call upon the spirits of water, the energy of the bear and salmon, to guide us in introspection, healing, and renewal. Welcome.

North direction

We invoke the North, the direction of night and ancestral wisdom. We call upon the spirits of the earth, the energy of the buffalo and deer, to offer us stability, knowledge, and protection. Welcome.

Mother earth (Pachamama)

We honor Mother Earth, who sustains and nurtures us. We ask for her blessing in this sacred circle and thank her for her abundance and generosity. Welcome.

Father sky

We honor Father Sky, the great spirit that embraces everything. We ask for his guidance, to enlighten our path and protect us with his infinite love. Welcome.

Heart center

We focus on the heart of the circle. May our intention be pure and our purpose clear. We unite in love and gratitude. Here and now, we are present.

10.2 Information about cacao

Once blessed, the Tlamanalli is activated, and you can perform the ceremony with confidence.

We will continue briefly sharing the origins of cacao and its journey to the present day.

We will briefly explain its name, the legend surrounding it, its composition, and the physical and spiritual benefits it offers.

It is important to mention that this is not the typical "hot chocolate" you drink at cafés or at home. This cacao is prepared in a pre-Hispanic or ancestral way, so its taste and texture may be different, even strange to some.

You should mention that if they do not like the flavor, they do not have to finish it. But they should take a few sips, savoring the cacao so that it can work its magic.

This moment sets the foundation for the depth and transformation that the cacao ceremony can offer, allowing each participant to connect with the spirit of cacao and the sacred purpose of the gathering.

We suggest keeping this part under 10 minutes. While the information about cacao is undoubtedly fascinating, participants are here to experience a direct connection with the spirit of cacao, not to listen to a lecture.

Additionally, all this information is easily available online, so it is more important to focus on the experiential aspect we offer.

10.3 Purpose of the ceremony

The purpose or theme of the ceremony is the heart of the experience.

It is crucial for the facilitator to clearly communicate the theme and guide the participants through activities that integrate and amplify this purpose.

Night-time outdoor cacao ceremony

The facilitator may decide if they want participants to close their eyes while delivering this information. This can help participants focus and connect more deeply with the purpose of the ceremony. The explanation should be clear and centered, providing a full understanding of the theme and its relevance.

10.4 Letting go of what we no longer need

Human beings tend to accumulate not just objects, but also emotions, beliefs, and behavioral patterns that, over time, limit us.

Some people never get rid of anything, turning their homes into a kind of storage room where, ironically, they never find what they are looking for. Others cling to rigid ideas, refusing to listen to any argument that might challenge their status quo, out of fear that everything they know will collapse.

There are also those who, after years of living with an illness, seem to resist healing because the illness has given them a role that earns them the attention of others. And finally, many remain loyal to behavioral family patterns that only limit them, without knowing where to begin transforming them.

In the cacao ceremony, we dedicate time for participants to recognize that everything which no longer serves them can be transmuted. We carry out simple exercises to release those burdens that prevent us from moving forward.

Usually, it is suggested to release something related to the theme of the celebration. For example, if the ceremony focuses on connecting with gratitude, you may want to release pride, a behavior that prevents you from being grateful by making you feel superior.

One option is to write on a piece of paper an affirmation like: "Here and now, I decree that, from today, I release pride and open myself to gratitude." At the end of the ceremony, you can burn or bury the paper, symbolizing your intention to release that burden and allow the universe to receive your desire for transformation.

You can also use the Ho'oponopono technique, repeating three times the words "I love you," "I'm sorry," "Please forgive me," and "Thank you," focusing on how you behave with pride. This technique will help dissolve the root of that behavior.

10.5 Integration of the purpose

Once we've released what was preventing us from fully enjoying the theme of the ceremony, we move on to integrating its essence and deeply connecting with its meaning. This can include:

Awareness exercise:

> Facilitating introspection so participants can reflect and, if they wish, share their thoughts.

Breathwork:

> Breathing techniques to center and calm the mind, aligning participants with the energy of the purpose.

Dance:

> Free or guided movement to release tension and connect with the body.

Guided meditation:

> A specific meditation related to the theme of the ceremony.

It is important to note that the chosen activities may vary depending on the purpose and length of the ceremony. There is no one-size-fits-all approach, as each ceremony has a different goal and, therefore, requires a different approach.

For example, a cacao ceremony meant to release ancestral energies will be quite different from one to welcome a baby. The activities should be adapted to the specific needs and energies of each occasion. Some ideas include:

Releasing ancestral energies:

- Forgiveness and reconciliation exercises.
- Emotional release dynamics.
- Rituals of connection and honoring ancestors.

Welcoming a baby:

- Celebration and joyful activities.
- Blessings and well-wishes to the newborn.
- Expression of gratitude and welcoming the new life.

Each ceremony should be designed with a specific goal in mind, ensuring the selected activities are appropriate and meaningful for the context and the participants.

In this QR you'll find the script for one of our most beloved and frequently shared ceremonies: THE GRATITUDE CACAO CEREMONY as well as extra content selected to help you plan, guide, and deepen your own experiences

You can also access it from:

https://thewingbook.com/en/bonus/cacao-ceremony/

10.6 Presenting cacao into the ceremony

Right after finishing the activities related to the ceremony's purpose and having released and settled what was necessary, the facilitator will present the cacao.

The cacao may have been prepared beforehand, brought to the circle while songs are sung, or it can be prepared in front of the participants, accompanied by chants, humming, or simply playing the selected music for that moment.

When both of us are present at the ceremony, we like that while one of us prepares the cacao, the other plays the chosen instruments for the occasion and sings appropriate chants. Then, we invite participants to sing a chorus with us before serving the cacao.

In the chapter on the "Ceremonial Cacao Recipe," we detail everything related to the formula, cooking, and presentation of the cacao. In the chapter on "Sacred Music," you will find the appropriate music for the ceremony.

10.7 How to serve the cacao

It is well known that, symbolically, we receive from the left side, which is feminine and passive, and we give from the right side, which is masculine and active.

Therefore, once you have the ceremonial cacao ready, it is time to use a ladle to fill the cups of cacao and hand them to the participants, starting with the person to your right.

We know from the work of Dr. Masaru Emoto the power that spoken words have, so our intention is to fill each cup of cacao with wonderful wishes and positive energy.

We wait until all participants have their cup of cacao between their hands, and once everyone is ready, we encourage them to declare aloud a positive quality to infuse their cup: love, joy, abundance, wisdom, among others.

This gesture fosters a sense of unity and community among the participants, as each one contributes their energy for individual and collective well-being.

10.8 Cacao drinking ritual

Drinking the cacao is one of the final activities of the ceremony and should be done with full reverence.

Invite the participants to hold their cup with both hands, bringing it to their heart for a few seconds, connecting with the energy of the cacao.

Encourage participants to drink mindfully and with gratitude, savoring each sip while feeling how the cacao warms their body and expands their heart.

Clarify that it is not necessary to finish the entire cup, and if they want more, they can have it, as there is enough cacao for everyone.

Before they begin drinking, share a few words to remind them of the intention and benefits of drinking the cacao. Here are a few examples you can use:

Consciously drinking cacao

Thank you, spirit of cacao, for the love and blessings you give us. In today's gathering, we ask for your guidance and abundance so that our intention_____ (insert the intention of the ceremony) may be fulfilled.

We thank you, spirit of cacao, for the love and blessings you offer us. In today's ceremony, we ask for your support and generosity to achieve our intention_____ (insert the intention of the ceremony)

Thank you spirit of cacao, for your love and blessings. Today we ask for your support and protection to reach our intention of....

Allow time for reflection and integration while you sing medicine songs, or if you prefer, play your selected playlist. Feel the energy of the group to determine the appropriate amount of time. However, 5 minutes of meditative state may be enough.

CHAPTER 11

CLOSING THE CACAO CEREMONY

11.1 Invitation to choose an oracle card

Before concluding the cacao ceremony, invite your participants to select an oracle card from those around the Tlamanalli. Explain that each person has arrived at this moment for a special reason, and the chosen card is no coincidence. This message or guidance is exactly what they need to achieve greater harmony in their lives.

Suggest that participants take a photo of their card, allowing them to reflect on its message over time and deepen their understanding and wisdom. This practice will help them integrate the guidance received during the ceremony.

11.2 Sharing ceremony experience

Once all participants have chosen their card and are seated quietly, invite them to share their experiences, feelings, emotions, and reflections.

Don't force anyone to speak, but mention that, due to time constraints, each person will have a maximum of 5 minutes to share. Signal the end of the time ringing a small bell or any other element you find appropriate.

This space is highly valued in the ceremony, as participants are in a high state of mind and often wish to share their feelings and gratitude.

11.3 Closing the Tlamanalli

At the end of the celebration, and before participants leave, it is time to close the Tlamanalli. The facilitator will thank each element representing the cardinal points and all the spiritual beings and guides that were present during the ceremony.

You can create your own thank you prayer, but here is one we frequently use and which we adapt to each ceremony.

> *We thank the presence of the elementals of water, fire, air, and earth, as well as the angels, archangels, spiritual guides, and beings of light who have accompanied and supported us in this beautiful cacao celebration.*
>
> *We also want to thank you all for coming and participating in making this celebration a moment of love and inspiration.*
>
> *We say goodbye with love and appreciation, carrying the blessings and harmony we have received in our hearts. Thank you all!*

11.4 Saying goodbye to participants

Once the rituals are finished, it is time to close and bid farewell to the participants.

We recommend that this final contact be thoughtfully prepared as well, so that participants leave with a good impression of the event and your care for them.

Before the participants leave, make sure that each of them is in perfect condition to begin the journey home. Check that their pupils are not dilated.

If so, it's important to do grounding exercises, such as standing up and gently stamping their feet on the ground. Additionally, invite them to drink rose water, because it contains the energy of love and helps them stay present and protected.

It's helpful to inform them that they might have all sorts of dreams, as the brain is processing and rearranging what has been shifted during the ceremony. There's no need to worry, as the body is wise and, within a maximum of 24 hours, it will realign all their energy, so they feel whole and can function perfectly in their daily life.

However, if you feel that topics have arisen that might be worth exploring, we advise seeking a professional to work through them. Everything that surfaces, which was hidden in the subconscious, comes up because it is time to work on it, and by releasing it, you allow yourself to reach a higher level of awareness.

When we take a leap in consciousness, we perceive our environment, relationships, and life from a new perspective, which grants us deeper understanding, a greater sense of purpose, and an unmatched inner peace. This transformation allows us to feel more connected with the universe and to experience authentic, lasting happiness.

11.5 Gift for participants

At every ceremony, there is a small gift as a reminder of what has taken place, and participants receive it with honor and gratitude.

Participants receive a gift at the end of the ceremony

These gifts are chosen based on their connection to one of the following motives:

- The intention of that ceremony

- Relationship with the environment

- Relationship with cacao

- Relationship with LOVE

- Relationship with the type of participants

Here are some ideas for offerings you can give to your participants

- A small bag with 7 roasted cacao beans so they can take one each day and stay connected to the spirit of cacao.
- A tumbled rose quartz for them to carry with them, helping them stay in touch with love and self-acceptance. A person who loves and accepts themselves can love and accept others.
- A flyer with the dates of upcoming celebrations or courses you will be offering.
- A small notebook for them to jot down thoughts that may arise post-ceremony.

11.6 Product sales

Participants often become enamored with some of the objects displayed on the Tlamanalli, such as cards, feathers, candles, stones, etc.

It's beneficial for both you and them to have some of these products available for sale, sparing them the task of searching for them in stores, and you also earn a small profit. It's a win-win!

11.7 Collect the ceremony materials

Once the attendees have left the room, you can begin to dismantle the altar.

Gather all disposable items, and ideally, we recommend burying them in a nearby field or park. If that's not possible, you can remove them and throw them away in the garbage bin.

Make sure to energetically cleanse the minerals and objects for future use. There are several ways to perform these cleansing. We like to use the 4096Hz tuning fork, as it's a very quick and effective method.

All you need to do is activate the tuning fork and place the tip on the mineral or object until it stops vibrating, doing this at least three times for each object and placing it on different parts of the item.

A WARM FAREWELL

Dear reader,

We've reached the end of this shared journey, a path filled with love, intention, and connection through cacao ceremonies. We hope you've found in these pages' information, practical guides, and inspiration to create and hold sacred spaces where healing and transformation can flourish.

Throughout this book, we have explored together the magic of cacao, its ancestral roots, and its ability to open hearts and unite souls. Every ceremony is a unique opportunity to connect with us and others, creating deep and meaningful bonds that transcend time and space.

Always remember that every gesture, every word, and every moment in a cacao ceremony holds the power to transform. The intention you put into each step, from preparing the space to the final farewell, is what makes these ceremonies so special and full of life.

We hope you carry with you that you have learned and apply it in your life and your own ceremonies, enriching both your path and those who join you. May your ceremonies continue to grow and bloom, bringing peace, joy, and healing to all who are fortunate enough to participate in them.

Each ceremony is a seed planted in the heart of the earth, and each one of us is a gardener of love and light.

Each person will find something unique in this book, something that resonates with their own experience and current stage of life.

Cacao doesn't impose itself; it approaches gently. It accompanies, supports, and reveals what is ready to be seen.

If these pages have opened questions, memories, or new ways of feeling, trust that movement. The path doesn't end here: it continues in every conscious gesture, in every ceremony, in every encounter with yourself.

Thank you for allowing the spirit of cacao to walk beside you. It has been an honor to share this journey.

With all our love and gratitude,

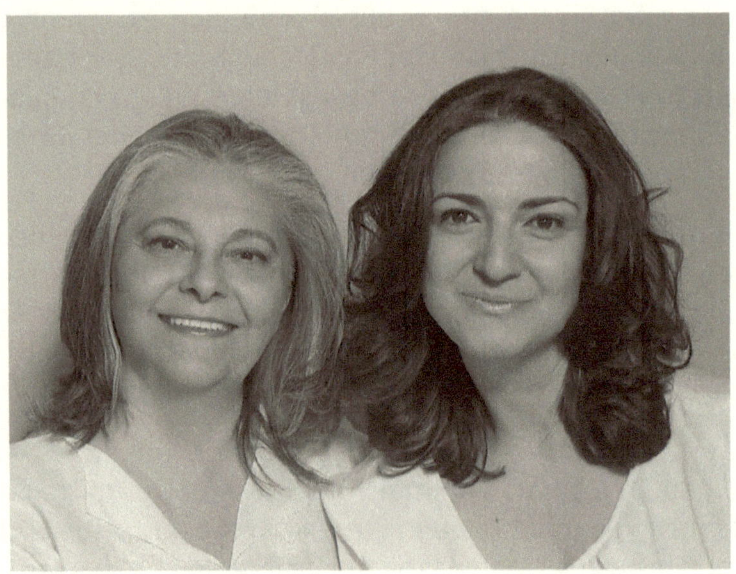

Mercedes Cadarso Sánchez..............Maria Socastro González

ADDITIONAL NOTE

If you wish to delve deeper into working with cacao, you can visit us at **www.cacaoschool.com.**

There you will find our 100% online **CACAO CEREMONY FACILITATOR** course, a comprehensive training program designed for those who feel called to guide others from a respectful, conscious, and well-founded perspective.

You can also discover the *Cacao Spirit* oracle cards, a tool lovingly created to accompany ceremonies or as a personal guide.

They are currently available in Spanish, but we are working to make them available in English as well.

In the above QR code we have compiled additional material specially created to expand and enrich your ceremonies: practical resources, suggestions, and content that complement this book and invite you to continue exploring. Hope you enjoy it!

You can also access it from:

https://thewingbook.com/en/bonus/cacao-ceremony/

REFERENCES

Emoto, Masaru (2004). The Hidden Messages in Water. Editorial La Liebre de Marzo.This book explores how human emotions and thoughts can influence the molecular structure of water. Its focus on vibration and intention is fundamental for understanding how conscious energy can affect natural elements, like water in cacao.

Cooper, Diana (2015). The New World: Spiritual Teachings for the New Age. Arkano Books.This book offers teachings on the new emerging spiritual energy and how to align ourselves with it. Its concepts can inspire the creation of a ceremonial environment elevated in vibration and purpose.

Van Durme, Monique (2010). Shamanic Rituals: A Practical Guide to Spirituality in Harmony with Nature. Editorial Obelisco. This work provides tools for rituals connected to nature, offering inspiration to integrate natural and symbolic elements into cacao ceremonies.

Shulman, C. Michael (2006). Cacao and Chocolate: History and Culture of the New World Seed. University of Arizona Press.A deep vision of the history of cacao and its cultural significance, useful for framing ceremonies within their ancestral context and understanding the sacred relationship many cultures have with cacao.

Dispenza, Joe (2017). Breaking the Habit of Being Yourself: How to Lose Your Mind and Create a New One. Editorial Urano. A book that explores how our beliefs and thoughts shape our reality. Ideal for facilitators who wish to integrate consciousness work and mental transformation into cacao ceremonies.

Swan, Teal (2016). The Completion Process: The Practice of Putting Yourself Back Together Again. Gaia Ediciones. A deep approach to understanding and transforming emotions, ideal for facilitators who wish to help participants integrate and process their experiences during cacao ceremonies.

Judith, Anodea (2016). Wheels of Life: A User's Guide to the Chakra System. Arkano Books. This book on the chakras offers an energetic perspective that can be applied to cacao ceremonies, helping facilitators balance participants' energies during the ritual.

Haramein, Nassim (2010). The Holofractographic Universe. Independent Research. Although not a traditional book, Haramein's ideas about the interconnectedness of the entire universe can provide a philosophical and energetic foundation for those facilitating ceremonies focused on unity and unconditional love.

Wilber, Ken (2006). The Spectrum of Consciousness. Editorial Kairós. This book explores levels of consciousness from a transpersonal psychology perspective, helping facilitators work with different mental and spiritual states in the context of cacao ceremonies.

Dyer, Wayne (2004). The Power of Intention: Learning to Co-create Your World Your Way. Editorial Grijalbo. A book that explores how conscious intentions can influence the creation of our reality, applicable to the preparation and development of cacao ceremonies, where intention plays a fundamental role.

Hawkins, David R. (2002). Power vs. Force: The Hidden Determinants of Human Behavior. Hay House. This book introduces the concept of levels of consciousness, a scale that classifies states of consciousness from the most destructive to the most elevated.

Josaya (2011). Ho'oponopono. Editorial Sirio. A clear and concise book on the Hawaiian Huna technique, which helps release limiting beliefs and thoughts in minutes. You can teach this technique during ceremonies to clear blockages.

Cadarso, Victoria (2012). Embrace Your Inner Child. Editorial Palmyra. The inner child is the key to accessing our most vulnerable emotions, and a facilitator working with this approach can create more transformative and connected ceremonies.

Cadarso, Mercedes & Gonzalez Maria Socastro (2025). Sound Therapy (Revised edition) The Wing Book - Complete manual on how to use sound frequencies in therapies or rituals.

Cadarso, Mercedes & Gonzalez Maria Socastro (2026). The Spirit of Cacao, 44 Oracle Cards-Arkano Books - These cards can be used at any time, but in cacao ceremonies, their power is amplified, transmitting messages that align the heart and spirit with the energy of cacao.